T0270192

THE
SIX BARDOS
OF THE
TIBETAN BOOK
OF THE DEAD

THE
SIX BARDOS
OF THE TIBETAN
BOOK OF THE DEAD

Dzogchen Teachings on
the Peaceful and Wrathful Deities

A Sacred Planet Book

**Ven. Khenchen Palden Sherab Rinpoche
and Ven. Khenpo Tsewang Dongyal Rinpoche**

Edited by members of the Samye
Translation Group: Craig Bialick, Lama
Pema Dragpa, and Amanda Lewis

Inner Traditions
Rochester, Vermont

Inner Traditions
One Park Street
Rochester, Vermont 05767
www.InnerTraditions.com

SUSTAINABLE FORESTRY INITIATIVE   Certified Sourcing
www.forests.org
SFI-00854

Text stock is SFI certified

Sacred Planet Books are curated by Richard Grossinger, Inner Traditions editorial board member and cofounder and former publisher of North Atlantic Books. The Sacred Planet collection, published under the umbrella of the Inner Traditions family of imprints, includes works on the themes of consciousness, cosmology, alternative medicine, dreams, climate, permaculture, alchemy, shamanic studies, oracles, astrology, crystals, hyperobjects, locutions, and subtle bodies.

Copyright © 2024 by Padmasambhava Buddhist Center

This work was previously published in 2012 as Part II of *The Essential Journey of Life and Death, Volume 1: The Indestructible Nature of Body, Speech, and Mind* by Dharma Samudra Publishing Company

All rights reserved. No part of this book may be reproduced or utilized in any form or by any means, electronic or mechanical, including photocopying, recording, or any information storage and retrieval system, without permission in writing from the publisher.

Cataloging-in-Publication Data for this title is available from the Library of Congress

ISBN 979-8-88850-129-0 (print)
ISBN 979-8-88850-130-6 (ebook)

Printed and bound in the United States by Lake Book Manufacturing, LLC
The text stock is SFI certified. The Sustainable Forestry Initiative® program promotes sustainable forest management.

10   9   8   7   6   5   4   3   2   1

Text design by Priscilla Baker and layout by Kenleigh Manseau
This book was typeset in Garamond Premier Pro with Trade Gothic LT Std and Hypatia Sans Pro used as display typefaces
All gonpa wall and mural photographs are used with permission
© Padmasambhava Buddhist Center
Photo of His Holiness Dudjom Rinpoche on facing page by Les Levine, New York City, 1975.
Photo of Venerable Khenchen Palden Sherab Rinpoche on facing page by Derek Sarno, West Palm Beach, Florida, 2008
Photo of Lama Chimed Namgyal on facing page by Mimi Bailey, West Palm Beach, Florida, 1994

To contact or learn more about the Padmasambhava Buddhist Center visit
padmasambhava.org.

❧

This book is dedicated to the memory of
His Holiness Dudjom Rinpoche,
Venerable Khenchen Palden Sherab Rinpoche,
Lama Chimed Namgyal, and all the lineage holders
of these secret teachings, as well as all the devoted
practitioners of the past, present, and future.

His Holiness Dudjom
Rinpoche (1904–1987)

Venerable Khenchen
Palden Sherab Rinpoche
(1938–2010)

Lama Chimed
Namgyal
(1913–2001)

Contents

APPENDICES

❧

Acknowledgments

This book is a compilation of many years of oral teachings given by the Venerable Khenpo Rinpoches between the years 1991 and 2010. It would not have been possible without the devoted, generous efforts of many sangha members. Since so many people have helped transcribe and edit these teachings, the Samye Translation Group would like to thank everyone in the order that their contributions appear in this book.

Thanks to Paul Levy for the foreword.

The preface, spoken by the Venerable Khenpo Rinpoches on March 29, 2010, during the 2010 Seven Chapter Prayer monthlong Dzogchen retreat at Palden Padma Samye Ling, in upstate New York, was transcribed by Amanda Lewis and edited by Pema Dragpa and Amanda Lewis.

The "Introduction to the Six Bardos" by the Venerable Khenpo Rinpoches was taught in Portland, Oregon, on September 16, 2008, and was transcribed by Pema Dragpa and edited by Pema Dragpa and Amanda Lewis.

The practice known as Daka Yeshe Do, Meditation on Absolute Wisdom: The Moment of Death Sutra, found in the appendices, was translated by Venerable Khenpo Tsewang Dongyal Rinpoche, edited by Peter DeNiro, and prepared for layout by Pema Tsultrim. As always, we are deeply grateful to Lama Lorraine, Lama Pema Tsultrim, and Lama Pema Dragpa for their joyful and steadfast administrative help running the Padmasambhava Buddhist Center/Palden Padma Samye Ling. We would also like to thank the resident staff of Palden Padma Samye Ling, whose work actively supports the Venerable Rinpoches' activities both locally and internationally. And we further wish to extend our thanks to all members and friends of the Padmasambhava Buddhist Center worldwide for their constant support over many years.

Most importantly, we offer our heartfelt gratitude and devotion to the Venerable Khenpo Rinpoches for blessing us with the opportunity to receive and practice these profound teachings.

We request that Venerable Khenpo Tsewang Dongyal Rinpoche and the Yangsi reincarnation of Venerable Khenchen Palden Sherab Rinpoche continuously turn the wheel of Dharma, and we ceaselessly offer prayers for their long and healthy lives.

We sincerely ask the forgiveness of all wisdom beings, holders of the teachings, and readers for any and all errors and misinterpretations of the teachings present in this text, and we welcome suggestions on how to improve it in the future.

May everyone who reads this text understand the value and meaning of their precious human life, and may their highest aspirations be fulfilled for the benefit of all beings. May all beings understand the meaning of the true nature and attain supreme buddhahood.

Awakening to Our True Nature

By Paul Levy

'd like to start off this foreword by reflecting back to you, at least in my opinion, how fortunate—indeed, blessed—you are to have come across this book. These are authentic teachings, transmitted by realized teachers, whose sole purpose is to help liberate us from our mind-created prison and awaken us to our true nature so we can remember who we actually are.

The teachings contained in this book are not abstract theories or mere speculations; they are pure, unmediated instructions on how to realize our true nature that have been passed down through an unbroken lineage of enlightened masters going back thousands of years, to Shakyamuni Buddha, and to Guru Padmasambhava, the great eighth-century *siddha* regarded as the Buddha of our age, who concealed these teachings as a mind treasure, or *terma*, to be revealed at a later time when conditions are right. That time is now.

These teachings undo one little but enormously consequential mistake that all but the most enlightened among us unconsciously make:

in essence, as if falling under a spell, we have succumbed to the chronic habitual pattern of contracting against our own light and clinging to a false sense of a separate self, and this has fed a sense of lack and scarcity and a kind of existential insecurity about who we truly are. This is a form of grasping, a holding onto and becoming attached to the way our conditioned mind thinks and believes things—including ourselves—exist. It is a pattern that we continuously enact beneath our conscious awareness, which means it is rendered unconscious. Unless illumined and seen through, this dynamic develops into what in Buddhism is called "ego clinging." As a result, we invest much of our precious life force in identifying with, defending, and protecting this fictitious identity, this separate egoic self that doesn't even exist in the way that we've been imagining it does. As if weaving a cocoon around our own true nature, we unwittingly suffocate ourselves by identifying with this self-created egoic illusion, a process that endlessly generates a whole host of other illusions that become mutually self-reinforcing. No one is doing this to us—we are doing this to ourselves. This is the essence of the madness that afflicts the human species.

This is a great danger that Western psychiatrist C. G. Jung warned us about—to mistakenly identify with what he called the "fictive personality," a process that informs and gives shape to the collective insanity that is currently being enacted all over the world. This idea is supported by the revelations of quantum physics, which has been described as "the crowning intellectual achievement of the last century."* In essence, the wisdom that has been unlocked in discovering the quantum is comparable to the insights that the spiritual masters of the East have already realized. The teachings that Venerable Khenchen Palden Sherab Rinpoche and Venerable Khenpo Tsewang Dongyal Rinpoche, affectionately known by their students worldwide as "the Khenpo Rinpoches," are offering here transcend time, place, and culture and are truly universal. And even though Khenchen Palden Sherab Rinpoche passed away in 2010—notably only weeks after his final teachings, which are found in this book—his wisdom and compassion permeate the three times. His

---

*John Preskill, *Quantum Enigma*, QuantumEnigma website.

reincarnation, Khenchen Yangsi Rinpoche, was found in 2016 (the term *yangsi* is used to refer to the reincarnation of a master).

The dynamic that fuels the ongoing creation and maintenance of this false identity, whose origin and cure is to be found nowhere except within our own minds, drives us into a state of delusion in which we become disoriented and deranged, thereby obscuring the awareness of our true nature. These teachings reveal us exactly as we are, which is to say they reveal our true nature, which is always with us and is already liberated. They help us open our spiritual eyes so that we can finally see, thus healing the chronic, self-induced psychospiritual blindness that afflicts our species.

I have had the honor of knowing and studying with the Khenpo Rinpoches for about forty years. Connecting with these masters has truly been one of the greatest blessings of my life. After meeting the Khenpos I remember feeling so incredibly fortunate, like I had won the lottery a trillion times over. Not quite able to believe my good fortune in finding beings like the Khenpos living in the middle of the samsara that is New York City, I took full advantage of their availability, trying my best to do the practices they taught, which literally transformed my life, leading me to find both my vocation as well as myself. I feel true joy and happiness in being able to share with you what has helped heal and transform my own life.

When I first met the Khenpo Rinpoches in 1984, I was going through a particularly difficult time in my life. They never turned down my seemingly endless requests to meet with them (typically every week), offering me support in every way they possibly could, even going out of their way if they thought it would help. At a meeting with some of my fellow students years later, I shared how the Khenpos had quite literally saved my life. I quickly realized that I wasn't the only one in the room whose lives they—and their teachings—had saved. The teachings they offer—the nectar of Dharma—can be likened to life-giving oxygen for the soul.

I am of the opinion that one of the Khenpos' *siddhis*, which can be conceived of as being superhero powers that are the result of realization, is their incredible ability to teach and transmit the Dharma. I have personally received teachings from great masters of many different traditions, but have never received such direct, embodied, psycho-activating transmissions—as if from one heart and mind to another—as when the Khenpos teach the Dharma. The Khenpos are considered to be two of the greatest scholar-practitioners in all of Tibetan history. In my mind they are the personification of the archetype of the enlightened teacher in human form. I think of them as a two-headed bodhisattva whose sole raison d'etre for being on this planet at this time is to help humanity wake up and remember who we are.

Years ago, when the Khenpos were visiting me in Portland, Oregon, I set up teachings for them that I had advertised as "teachings and transmissions." As we were driving to one of the venues, I reminded them that they were not only to give a teaching, they were also supposed to give a transmission. As soon as I said this, the Khenpos broke into hysterical laughter. I immediately "got the transmission" and realized the absurdity of what I had just said. Because they had so consciously integrated and realized their own true nature, their very physical presence, along with their teachings, *was* the transmission! In other words, they so embodied the Dharma teachings about our true nature, which is all about love, compassion, and wisdom, that they effortlessly and naturally could transmit their realization in each and every moment. In essence, the Khenpo Rinpoches had become transparent to the divine light that shines through all of us—what they call "the sunlight of our inborn nature of primordial wisdom." The light of this realization is available to each and every one of us if we but have the eyes to see.

I've had other lamas who knew the Khenpos tell me that in Tibet they are thought of as living buddhas. The word *buddha* means one who has awakened to the dreamlike nature of reality. This is to say that a buddha is someone who has awakened to the empirical reality that this universe is a shared collective dream that we—all of us—are dreaming into material form moment by moment. To the extent that we are asleep to our true nature, however, we are instead using our innate power to create our experience against ourselves instead of in service to ourselves. Awakening to the dreamlike nature of ourselves and our situation and discovering our true nature is the medicine needed for the collective insanity that ails our species.

Though Khenchen Rinpoche left his body in 2010, his living spirit comes through the teachings in this book so strongly that it is as if he is fully present with us as we read his words. These very teachings are a form of his subtle body and spiritual legacy that he has left behind for our benefit. There is a sense that linear time has collapsed between the time when he gave these teachings and this very "now" moment. In reading his words, we are—potentially, depending on how open we are—receiving a living transmission directly from his realization into our minds.

The Khenpo Rinpoches are masters of our times, two holders of the Dzogchen ("Great Perfection") lineage, which is considered to be the supreme, ultimate, and simplest path to liberation in the Buddhadharma. I am of the opinion that the arrival of Dzogchen teachings in the West is the most profound spiritual event that has happened in our world in two thousand years—an event that has as its scientific equivalent the emergence of quantum physics in the early twentieth century. The Dzogchen teachings are not ordinary Buddhist teachings. Dzogchen is not an ordinary practice, and yet it couldn't be more natural. Because of their psychospiritual power, these teachings were kept secret until relatively recently. Like a time-released hidden treasure, or *terma*, these teachings are being revealed and shared at the exact moment in time when they are most needed by the world.

In Dzogchen, there is nothing to purify, nothing to transform, nothing to liberate, nothing to exorcise, and literally nothing to do other than recognize and then rest and abide in our true nature. One morning over breakfast, as if giving me a personal transmission, Khenchen Palden Sherab Rinpoche simply said to me, "My one practice is to not get distracted." This is Dzogchen in a nutshell: recognize our intrinsically pure nature and don't forget it. This is true anamnesia (the opposite of amnesia)—an "unforgetting" not of a past historical event, but a remembering of something timeless that partakes in the eternal that exists within each of us in every moment.

Dzogchen, the "Diamond Vehicle" (*vajra* translates as "diamond"), is the pinnacle of the Vajrayana tradition and is also known as "Tantrayana." In laying the foundation for the realization of our true nature, practitioners of this tradition do practices such as reciting mantra and visualizing deities, thereby engaging their body, speech, and mind. Though the countless variety of tantric deities looks just like the polytheism of old, these deities are not seen as external figures that the practitioner believes in and worships, but rather are understood as representing the diverse qualities of the enlightened mind. To use the language of psychology, these various deities symbolize the multifaceted archetype of the Self, our own deepest and most true nature.

In tantra we focus our attention on the archetypal image of the deity and identify with it in order to arouse the awakened aspects of ourselves, bringing these qualities into our present reality. In these visualization practices, the practitioner is instructed to not just see the visualized deity that symbolizes our enlightened nature as being outside of and separate from ourselves, but to merge with the essential qualities of the deity, thereby identifying with the deity to the point where we creatively imagine ourselves as being the deity itself. This is why tantra is also referred to as "deity yoga." In doing so, we are tuning in to and helping to bring forth in ourselves what the deity symbolically represents—the part of us that is already healed, whole, and awake.

Some of these deities are in sexual union—called *yab-yum*—which can easily mislead the uninitiated reader to mistakenly think Buddhist tantra is about sexual techniques, without realizing that these tantric deities represent the union of opposites, the coming together of the masculine and feminine parts of ourselves. This is none other than the *hieros gamos* of alchemy, the sacred marriage, which symbolizes the wholeness of our being. The practice of tantra is a powerful method to swiftly attain the state whereby we can serve and be of maximum benefit to all beings. Tantra helps us realize that the peaceful and wrathful deities mentioned in the title of this book—which we will invariably encounter in what is called the bardo of death—are ultimately nothing more than projections of our own mind. Once recognized as such, these deities reveal themselves to be the very means for our liberation. In essence, tantra is all about helping us wake up and become lucid in the dream of waking life.

These practices help us realize that our very sense of identity, being a function of our creative imagination and a construct of (i.e., something constructed by) our mind, is malleable. In our evocation, visualization, and identification with the deity, we are not merely creating a fabrication, imagining something that doesn't exist or isn't real, but rather through an act of creative imagination we are skillfully getting in touch with and becoming familiar with our always available and already existing enlightened nature. The view of Vajrayana is that within our deepest selves we are already perfect, complete, whole, and enlightened. These visualization practices are a way of dissolving our limited conception of ourselves in order to get in touch with—and embody—who we truly are, our buddha nature.

At the end of the visualization practice we are instructed to dissolve the visualization of the deity as ourself, for this can easily become a subtle form of ego-clinging and inflation, at which point we have arrived at the doorway to the state of Dzogchen, the open-ended, spacious emptiness and intrinsic freedom of our true nature. These visualization practices are thus the skillful means by which we creatively and consciously engage with the natural projective tendencies of the mind. On the one hand, projections in our day-to-day lives create separation between people. Our unconscious projections on others, for example, get in the way of our seeing them as they really are. In Tibetan Buddhism, visualization practices consciously take advantage of our natural tendency to project the unknown parts of ourselves outside of ourselves. Just as psychology teaches us to withdraw our unconscious projections and find their source within ourselves, in these visualization practices we are instructed to recognize that the visualized deity is, like a mirror, reflecting back to us the awakened part of ourselves. We are invited to own and step into what the deity is symbolically revealing to us, a process that helps us deepen our intimate connection with our awakened nature, which has always been with us.

The Khenpo Rinpoches lived through their own hellish, harrowing, life-and-death ordeal of escaping Tibet during the Chinese invasion in 1959. They were refugees in India for many years before coming to the United States in 1984, which is to say that the Khenpos have known and experienced the suffering of samsara firsthand. Talking about their status as longtime refugees, the elder Khenpo, Khenchen Palden Sherab Rinpoche, one day said to me, "Everywhere I go is my home," which is a perfect expression of having found the ultimate refuge of his true nature within himself.

The Dzogchen realization is said to "cure the disease of effort," which implies that not only is there no effort involved in this realization, but that effort is itself the obscuration. Meeting the Khenpos makes this statement understandable, as they are always completely relaxed, at ease in the moment, just simply being themselves, living and being in the fullness of the natural state of what it is to be an authentic, openhearted human being. They are simply in service to the field of consciousness that we all share, modeling the very opposite of being anxious and stressed-out in a world gone mad. The congruence and coherence of their very being and the teachings they share offer us a doorway into that same state, a state that is always freely available to us. After all, it is our very nature that the Khenpos are effortlessly pointing to, reflecting at us, embodying, and transmitting.

The teachings contained in this book are pointing at the dreamlike nature of the universe while simultaneously being an expression of that very dreamlike nature at which they are pointing. As the Khenpos say again and again, "Everything is a dream." They counsel us to deeply reflect on the dreamlike nature of our situation. Why? In their own words, "Because it's really true." From the perspective of the teachings, which reveal the dreamlike nature of our situation in this and every moment, you, dear reader, have dreamed up these very teachings so as to potentially awaken yourself! But as the teachings state, you have to implement, put into practice, actualize, and bring into the core of your heart these teachings in order for them to effectively reveal your true nature. And what is our true nature? To quote the Khenpo Rinpoches, "Our nature is love. Our nature is compassion. Our nature is intelligence. Our nature is wisdom. Our nature is beautiful, and we're going to bring that up. This is known as 'practice.'"

It is not an accident that these profound and liberating teachings you now hold in your hands have appeared within the waking dream you are currently having. From the point of view of the teachings themselves, this can only be because of previous virtuous activities on your part that have paved the way for you to connect with such wisdom. My only advice is to take full advantage of your incredibly good fortune. Receive the teachings into your heart and do the practice—bring up and share with the world your beautiful inner heart qualities of love and compassion.

I can only imagine how our world would be utterly transformed as more people take in and earnestly practice the teachings contained in this book. These teachings are quite literally the medicine that can heal our world. Change in our world, however, truly starts with the individual, with each one of us. As the teachings themselves point out, our life—just like a dream—is ephemeral and impermanent. Why not make the most of the precious opportunity that life in the form of these truly sacred teachings is offering to us? As the Khenpo Rinpoches say, "Now is the time to ignite our inner light." What could possibly be more important than accomplishing what we are here to do—to realize who we truly are and let our light shine so that we can help others do the same.

Paul Levy has been a student of the Khenpo Rinpoches for forty years. He is the author of six books, including three books on the wetiko mind-virus and *The Quantum Revelation*.

Note to the Reader on Terminology and Lineage

This book includes terms specific to Vajrayana Buddhist practice that may not be familiar to some readers. The editors have made every attempt to clarify such terms in the text; the glossary at the end of the book also provides helpful explanations and expansions.

This book contains precious lineage teachings on living and dying that are beneficial to anyone interested in living a fuller, healthier life.

The Zhitro meditation instructions come from Buddha Shakyamuni and Guru Padmasambhava and have been continued in an unbroken lineage of Tibetan Buddhist scholars and meditators for centuries. Everyone is warmly invited to study these profound teachings, which constitute a profound lineage blessing by two of our greatest contemporary masters. And to receive even greater benefit from these teachings, the reader is encouraged to connect with a qualified lama to receive personal instructions on how to practice the profound meditation techniques mentioned in this book that have come down to us via lineage masters that go all the way back to Guru Padmasambhava and Buddha Shakyamuni.

Preface

This preface was transcribed from the Venerable Khenpo Rinpoches' first teaching at the 2010 spring Dzogchen retreat at Padma Samye Ling on the Seven Chapter Prayer by Guru Padmasambhava.

Generally speaking, the principal beneficial activity of the Buddha is teaching. The great teacher Buddha Shakyamuni gave teachings in order to wake up all sentient beings and dispel the hindrances that have bothered us for such a long time. These negativities will not just go away or be cleared up by anything except through teachings on love, compassion, and wisdom. For this reason in Buddhism it is often said that the Buddha will never wash our obscurations with water, sweep them up with a broom, or pick them up and put them in some place of liberation. Only by receiving teachings on the true nature can we clear away our dilemmas and hindrances.

Why can't the Buddha wash away our difficulties? Each of us has to recognize our own nature; every living being has to "click" their own mind. We create our own negative emotions; our own actions stain our minds, so only we can clear them away. The Buddha can show us skillful techniques and methods that will remove the cause of our troubles, but we ourselves have to apply these methods for them to work. The teachings are the conditions that tame our minds and make us ready to clear away the stains of duality.

By joining our effort together with the teachings of Buddha Shakyamuni and Guru Padmasambhava, we can change and wake ourselves up inside. To activate and sizzle these conditions we have to bring up our devotion, joy, and compassionate thoughts for all beings. All of these qualities begin from within. Once the blessings of the Buddha's teachings combine with our devotion, interest, and warm heart, it creates such a great powerful force to eliminate our suffering. The dark, cold duality that has been with us for so many years will begin to melt away.

This is known as "receiving blessings." The blessings of the teachings penetrate us so easily when we prepare ourselves to receive them. Without preparing ourselves by developing our natural qualities of love and compassion, no matter how perfect the conditions are and no matter how many blessings are reaching out to us from the Buddha and other great enlightened beings, they're not going to absorb into us or benefit us very much—they will just kind of go away. It's like when a pot is upside down—no matter how much water we pour in it, it's not going to fill up—the water just falls away. Similarly, if the pot is open just a little bit, then just a little bit of water stays inside. Devotion is our joy and appreciation. It is our respect and confidence and the warm, close feelings we have toward the teachings and the lineage. Devotion is a deep appreciation for our situation and for the opportunity to apply the teachings and share our goodness qualities with others. Love and compassion are truly so special. Ignite your devotion and combine it with genuine feelings of kindness and love that radiate to every living being. Without devotion, there's nowhere we can go, because devotion is the recognition and trust in our own goodness qualities and how we glorify and share them with others.

Eventually our interest, joy, and appreciation blossom so much that they develop into confident and unfailing devotion, which is so deep and powerful. By using our reasoning and the experience and knowledge we gain by applying the teachings, we develop a confidence in our own goodness qualities and in the genuine goodness of others. We really feel that this is how our nature is, and we want to express our true nature of love and compassion without any fear or hesitation. Based on this understanding, we begin to engage in the teachings with an incredible sense of joy and appreciation. When we have this kind of devotion, realization and the blessings of the Buddha and Guru Padmasambhava come so easily. Their blessings directly enter our hearts and minds, and our realization grows very quickly and naturally. As we continue to apply the teachings, eventually we will cultivate this kind of devotion, and then even a simple Dharma teaching will become so powerful and strong, and we will progress very well.

VEN. KHENCHEN PALDEN SHERAB RINPOCHE AND
VEN. KHENPO TSEWANG DONGYAL RINPOCHE
PADMA SAMYE LING
MARCH 29, 2010

Introduction to the Six Bardos

This introduction to the six bardos by the Venerable Khenpo Rinpoches was taught in Portland, Oregon, on September 16, 2008, and was transcribed by Pema Dragpa and edited by Pema Dragpa and Amanda Lewis.

B uddhism is a teaching of nonviolence, kindness, and compassion, as well as respect and appreciation for all living beings. Being harmonious and peaceful with everything that exists is the foundation of the entire teaching of Buddha Shakyamuni.

The great teacher Buddha Shakyamuni said that this is our true nature—these qualities are not new ideas or dogma that you bring into your life only when you practice Buddhism. Love, kindness, and compassion are the basic nature of every living being. When we connect with this nature, it is so soothing; we feel more calm and peaceful, and experience more joy and satisfaction. Therefore, as we practice and reflect on life, death, and dying, the Buddha always emphasized that we should ignite our basic goodness qualities of love, kindness, and compassion, which in Buddhism are known as *bodhichitta*, or the "mind of enlightenment." This will help us better understand the meaning of the natural rhythm and process of life and death.

The entire universe, including ourselves, is based on this nature. We never depart from this nature and we've never been apart from it. Everyone has this same basic nature—every tiny movement and everything in general moves according to this nature's rhythm and is a part of the natural process. In this way, life is natural, death is natural, and even the period after death is natural. These are all ongoing processes of the same nature. We should try to continually embrace all of the ways that this nature manifests without fear. When we accept this nature with confidence and joy, everything is seen as a beautiful process.

This entire natural system moves in cycles. We can see this when we look at the movements of day and night. If there is day, then definitely there will be twilight and nightfall. If there is night, there will be dawn, morning, and daylight. This process continues day after day and night after night, like a spiral. Similarly, winter, spring, summer, and autumn continually rotate into one another. When you look at all the cycles, from galaxies to our own bodies, every natural system is continually spiraling, breathing in and out, and then pausing before breathing in and out again. That is how the process of everything works. Buddha Shakyamuni said this throughout his teaching, and it was also taught by Guru Padmasambhava and all the other great practitioners and masters. Every system is a part of this nature. There is nothing outside of this nature. Everything exists within this framework, and we ourselves are also a part of it. It is not that this nature is on one side and we are on another side. We are part of this nature itself.

When we look at the external world, we see that everything goes through a similar process of birth, growth, and eventually an ending. But that is not the end of the process. If the perfect causes and conditions meet, new, rejuvenated qualities emerge from what has fallen apart, and the process continues. This happens with the seasons and plants and everything. Nothing ever actually ends. When something passes, it continues into the beginning of a new cycle.

Our life is the same. We take birth, grow up, and then die. According to Buddhism, death is not the end of life. In a way, death is the beginning of another era or chapter of life—we continue the process of life and death. Nothing ever really stops. As long as the right causes and conditions exist, everything continues—the light continues to spark without end. In Buddhism, this is known as *karma*. Karma never ends. In a way, karma is a continual chain reaction. The first moment is the cause and condition, and the next moment becomes the result. That very result becomes the cause and condition for the following moment. Each moment ignites and rejuvenates itself in a continual process that never ends. This is how we continually go through life after life. In brief, this is the general view of the process of life and death in Buddhism.

If we look at our own situation, our life began with our birth. According to Buddhism, this current life is not the first time we took birth; this is just one of many births we have taken in this world. We are in an ongoing process of life and death. Our birth in this life was not the first and will not be the last. It is just one of our births in a chain of births that has no beginning and no end. When we are born, what is it exactly that is taking birth? Consciousness takes birth. When our mind merges with the causes and conditions of our parents' red and white elements coming together, we are conceived. After conception, we go through a process of many different stages, every week growing and changing in our mother's womb. Then after about nine or ten months, we come out. This is normally known as "taking birth." We then continue to grow from being a baby until where we are now. We are currently in the process of living.

The next stage we will all go through is that of dying and death. According to Buddhism, the time to prepare for our death is right now. We should all begin preparing for this transition now because while we're in the process of dying it's difficult to begin making these preparations. So right now, while we're alive and well, is really the best time to prepare for the next transition or stage of life that we will have to face.

How do we prepare for our death and dying? The teachings always say that we should prepare by connecting to our true nature. This goodness nature is the nature of our mind. There are many different ways to connect with this nature, but we should just immediately go to our mind. The mind is what is going to travel when we die. Therefore we should make a close connection to the mind itself. That is the great preparation. Connecting to the mind means touching the true nature of the mind, which is love, kindness, compassion, joy, and confidence. These qualities are the true nature of the mind, so we should really become closely connected to them.

Loving-kindness and compassion are really so important. They are not important because religion says so. According to the Buddha, these qualities have nothing to do with religion—they are simply the true nature of the mind. Everybody appreciates love and compassion because they are natural qualities. Religion may talk about or emphasize these qualities a little more, but aside from that, love and compassion are really just the true nature of the mind. Therefore we should always connect our mind with its true nature of love and compassion. When we connect to these qualities, we feel a sense of genuineness in our hearts and minds. We feel more relaxed, more calm and peaceful. We also feel more satisfaction and joy. A very deep joy fills our heart and mind when we have thoughts of love, compassion, and kindness. We can see this for ourselves.

On the other hand, without joy, love, and compassion, even if we have everything else in the world, life seems kind of empty—nothing will give us a sense of complete satisfaction and joy. This is because we are not closely connected to our own true nature. Unnatural things cannot provide the same ultimate satisfaction as the beautiful qualities of our true nature. Therefore, loving-kindness and compassion are known as *bodhichitta*—the mind of enlightenment. Bodhichitta is the true nature of the mind. When we cultivate these qualities and feel more closely connected to them by doing more activities based on love and compassion, this is the best preparation for death and dying. It is also a great reward to ourselves—it feels good immediately and leads to final, ultimate joy as well. Sharing love and compassion is also a very special gift that we can give to others so that everyone is more joyful and happy. It's a great healing process. For these reasons, discovering the nature of our mind and sharing all of our beautiful natural qualities is very important on many levels and in many ways—for this life, for when we are dying, and for our life after death.

To touch this nature we must start with our mind. This is crucial. Each of us has a mind. It is intelligent and brilliant. It is beautiful, sparkling, and shining. It encompasses multiple colorful richness qualities. This is how the mind naturally is. The Buddha even said that it's impossible to explain all of the richness qualities of our mind. They are beyond our mundane conceptions. And we all have this richness; it's not something outside of what our own nature already is. In Buddhism, this basic, essential nature that we all have is known as *buddha nature*. When we reconnect to our basic nature, our mind becomes totally open, free, and infinite, like the sky. Yet if we look and try to find out what this mind is exactly, we cannot find our mind. The mind is nowhere. It is beyond time and space, beyond all limitations and boundaries. This is how the nature of our mind is right now. We're not talking about someone else's mind. We're talking about the mind of each and every one of us, and all of our minds are full of this richness.

So why aren't we already aware of the nature of our own mind? In a way, our mind is deluded. It is filled with grasping and ego-clinging, self-importance and negative emotions. These unnatural qualities are completely deluding and prevent us from beholding and recapturing the beautiful, rich nature of our mind.

Grasping makes our minds very narrow, partial, regimented, and very tight. The grasping mind always wants something else—whatever fits exactly with what the ego wants. But the true nature of mind is totally free and flexible. It is infinite and includes everything. Therefore, grasping and the true nature don't fit very well together. Right now we are almost totally occupied and controlled by grasping and ego-clinging, which doesn't agree with our true nature. Eventually, the true nature always takes over and grasping suffers. Grasping becomes sad and melancholy, and so we suffer. But that is not the true nature's fault. It is our mistaken grasping and ego-clinging that causes this. Grasping and ego-clinging don't like to accept natural changes because they are set on having everything their way. When our mind gets stuck like this, our true nature overruns us by following its natural flowing system, and so we begin to suffer.

Due to grasping, death can be very painful. If we refuse to accept the natural breathing rhythm of this process, as we die and even after death we can become very scared and uncertain. Otherwise, we will see death as just a transition or change, like day turning into night. Why are we clinging to the day and trying to avoid the night? The night will come. If we're always grasping day and don't want to experience twilight and night, what good does it do? Either way, night will come. We suffer because our grasping and ego-clinging don't like to accept or see change. They like to see things a certain way, and when it doesn't happen or when things change, that's when all the difficulties arise.

As we move closer to our true nature of acceptance, openness, freedom, love, and compassion, if we allow ourselves to be filled up with our true nature's beauty as it is, then everything in this life and after this life becomes a beautiful show of our true nature's rhythm. There is really nothing to be scared of, nothing that is alien or strange. It's all a part of the display of the nature of mind.

This beautiful nature is the nature of everything, including our mind. Our mind is naturally filled with love, compassion, and wisdom. These qualities are completely united. They are inseparable from one another. Love is emptiness, and emptiness is love. Compassion is emptiness, and emptiness is compassion. There is really no separation at all. Buddhism talks a lot about emptiness. Emptiness is not a vague, blank, negation state of mind. Emptiness is total freedom, infinity, and fullness. It is beyond all territories, limitations, and boundaries. It's not some icy, cold, hollow state. Emptiness is bursting with total freedom. Therefore, the Buddha taught that emptiness is loving-kindness, and loving-kindness is emptiness. Compassion is emptiness, and emptiness is compassion.

We can directly experience this by looking at our own mind. For example, when we talk about loving-kindness, where is that loving-kindness? When we look and try to find and grab that love, we cannot find any solid core existing in our experience of loving-kindness. That is emptiness. And yet, there is love, which is known as "appearance," or "clarity." The nature of our minds is so beautiful and special. When we closely connect to our true nature, we immediately experience total fearlessness. All of our doubts and hesitation instantly disappear. In their place we find total satisfaction, joy, and confidence arising within our mind. This is what we need to practice.

To practice means to closely connect to our true nature. In

Buddhism this is known as *meditation*. Meditation means abiding within our true nature, or being one with our own true nature. When we become familiar with our true nature and stay with that, we continue to carry that light now, during our dying process, and even after we pass away. That light never ends. Now is the time to ignite our inner light. Then our light of wisdom, love, and compassion will shine throughout all the changes that we go through. This is why the teachings always say to prepare for death and dying now while we have every opportunity. While everything in our situation is still under our control, we should prepare. If we wait until we're dying, then even if we want to prepare for death, the circumstances and conditions usually don't allow for that. It's very difficult to start then. Now we are free and have every opportunity, so we should begin right now.

Preparing for death with actual practice is very important to do now. Even though you may intellectually be familiar with these ideas, if you don't practice, your intellectual understanding and your actual experience of your own true nature remain separate. Whatever you learn intellectually, you must also absorb in your heart and mind. This is practice. As we all know, practice makes perfect, and even if it doesn't make it exactly perfect, practice will make it close to perfect!

In Tibetan, *bardo* means "intermediate state" or "period." There are three main intermediate states that we all go through: (1) birth and life, (2) dying and death, and (3) after death. Among these three periods— the bardo of life, the bardo of dying, and the bardo of death—we are currently in the bardo of life. Our next period is the bardo of dying, which will continue until we die.

Death is inevitable for everyone without exception. Since death is an essential part of nature's rhythm, everyone has to go through this, period. Everyone who is born has to experience dying and death, no matter how rich they are, how powerful they are, or how renowned they are. Even beings with the highest realization have to pass through the bardo of dying. This is just a passage that we all have to go through. If we experience the day, we will inevitably experience the night. No one is outside of these experiences—we cannot avoid them. This is just how nature moves.

Of course, we're not really telling you anything that you don't already know. Still, it's really important to reflect on why we die. Death is a part of nature. The immediate reason why we die is that our body declines as it grows older. The elements in our body don't have enough strength to hold together as a body. In Buddhism these elements are known as the five elements. They include earth, water, fire, wind, and sky or space. In a way, our physical body is a small example of these five elements, while the external world is a larger instance of the same five elements.

Buddhist cosmology describes how the external world also goes through these periods. Right now, the world seems very permanent, but it's not going to stay this way forever. It might stay together for aeons and aeons, but in the end it will fall apart. Similarly, our body is made of the five elements. When we are young, our body is very fresh, more tangible, and light. But as it gets older and declines, eventually it loses the strength to hold itself together and it falls apart. The teachings often say that the five elements will go back to the five elements, and consciousness will depart and take off. Currently, our mind resides within a physical body that is borrowed from the five elements. Our consciousness is like a tenant, and our body is like a house. Eventually, the house will decline until it completely falls apart, and then the resident mind will go on to the next bardo. This is the general idea of how the dying process unfolds.

While there are many different teachings about the body and the five elements, a simple way to explain this is that the flesh aspect of our body is the earth element, which goes back to the earth when we die. The liquid aspect of our body is the water element, which returns to the water element. The warmth of our body is the fire element, which goes back to the fire element. Our breathing is the wind element, and that returns to the wind. Our consciousness is part of the sky, or openness, and after it separates from our body it merges with space as it travels to the next stage. When the five elements of our body dissolve, the nutrition or energy of these elements completely merges into the outer five elements, and that is when we usually say that a person is dead.

On a subtler or more detailed level, the tantric teachings of Buddha Shakyamuni and Guru Padmasambhava say that even after our last breath we are still not completely dead. Right after our last breath, the white and red elements in our body lose their positions. At the moment of conception, our white element comes from our father, and our red element from our mother. The essences of these two elements reside in two different locations in our body. The essence of the red element mainly resides below our navel center. The essence of the white element mainly resides in the top of our head in the crown chakra. Right after our last breath, these two elements lose their positions: the white element's energy begins coming down, and the red element's energy moves up, until they meet in our heart center, where our consciousness becomes completely trapped by them. At the beginning of this life in our mother's womb our consciousness was also trapped by the white and red elements as we were conceived. Similarly, when we are dying, the essence energy of the two elements meets in our heart center, where they almost crush together, trapping our consciousness. This is the moment when a person is considered to be totally dead since the white and red elements have completely lost their positions in the body.

The bardo of dying concludes at the moment of death. During this process, the teachings often say that the dying person should connect more closely to their true nature by bringing up more love, compassion, wisdom, and confidence. You have to accept the situation. Don't let yourself be manipulated by ego-clinging, grasping, and duality mind. Embrace your true nature. Try not to be scared of this process—you have to accept it. If you've been practicing or have developed some faith during your life, you should ignite that faith. It doesn't matter what faith you have. You may be Buddhist or some other faith, but bring up your faith. This will support your confidence and affirm your destination.

This is the time to be more relaxed, settled, and confident. It's a bit like skydiving. You've never been skydiving, but it seems that after you've learned all the instructions and are in a plane with a parachute and everything is ready, when it comes to the final jump it's good to be confident—it's good to be happy and excited, and not scared and timid before your jump. Really, your practice of love and compassion and kindness is your parachute. Have joy and confidence, and bring up your faith and devotion. It's an exciting moment. You're moving forward in a beautiful way toward a beautiful destination. The teachings say that it's very important to activate all of your good qualities and not be scared.

If there are friends and family members around you, they should try not to create any kind of big emotional disturbances. Of course the death of a loved one is a very emotional time. But try not to be very sad and cry since it can disturb the person who is leaving. Try to generate more peace and harmony, and create a more relaxed atmosphere. All of this will really help the person taking this journey to transition more smoothly.

If you're a Buddhist practitioner and have made a close connection to the great nature during your life, the process of your death and dying provides tremendous opportunities for realization. The time right after the energies of the two elements join together and your consciousness is trapped in your heart center is usually very brief. It depends on the person, but it could be only a few seconds or a few minutes—either way, it won't last too long. Right after the energy of that joining force releases, at that moment your mind will experience the authentic nature, free from habitual patterns, free from any dogma, and free from any conceptions. It is brilliant like the autumn sky. This direct experience of the true nature dawns right then for everyone, but if you've been practicing Dzogchen or other great meditation techniques, then you'll be more likely to recognize the true nature. If you're able to merge your awareness with the realization of the true nature right then, you won't have to go through any further delusions in the bardo. At that moment you will reach enlightenment and connect to your buddha nature, which is to say the experience of complete realization.

The next bardo is the bardo of death. The bardo of death occurs between the moment of death and when you take rebirth. According to the Buddha, this period usually lasts an average maximum of about forty-nine days. Some people can stay one or two weeks, and after that they take rebirth, while others stay in this bardo for forty-nine days. In some cases, this state lasts for more than forty-nine days, but the average maximum of the bardo of death is forty-nine days.

What will our experience be like after we die and are in the bardo of death? Guru Padmasambhava said that it will be like a dream. It's not the same as life because there's no physical body or environment, but still your mental body goes through dreamlike experiences. What you experience depends on your past actions. In your lifetime, if you did good things that were connected with true love, compassion, and wisdom, then this bardo experience will be smooth, soothing, and overall more comfortable. If you did a lot of negative activities that caused suffering and created trouble and imbalance during your life, due to these negative habitual patterns in your mind your experiences will arise almost like mirror images of these activities, and your journey can be a little uncomfortable, restless, and frightening. You might experience this bardo more like a struggle. In any case, it's all just a dreamlike state. The dreamlike nature of this bardo doesn't really change, but according to the actions of previous lives, one dream may be smoother and the other rougher.

In any case, the experiences of the bardo of death do not exist outside of your mind. They are just imagined, self-reflected, dreamlike experiences without any solidity. They are mental imaginations or reflections. If you practiced Vajrayana techniques of visualizing buddhas and other forms of enlightenment during your life, when you experience the illusory displays of the bardo of death it will be very easy to connect to the imagined images and see them as your own self-display. If you immediately recognize that all of those experiences are just your mental imaginings, you will instantly stop rejecting and accepting them, and all of your feelings of hope and fear and doubt will cease. At that moment your awareness kind of wakes up and you experience sudden realization, and all of your deluded displays end. By connecting to the luminous blissfulness of enlightenment in this way, you realize the buddha nature.

The forty-nine-day period of the bardo of death is not the end. After this, consciousness takes rebirth according to its karma, or previous actions. The habitual force of the mind draws us to take rebirth, wherever that might be. The moment of our rebirth begins with conception and taking birth, and from there the process goes on and on. This is how the process of birth, death, and dying continues. Before taking rebirth, meditation practitioners have another opportunity to reach sudden enlightenment. If you have developed a good practice during your previous life, as you take rebirth you will have some control in choosing your destination and some of the circumstances of your rebirth. Instead of being controlled entirely by karma, your own intelligence will consciously choose your rebirth. In so doing you are connecting to the outreaching compassion of the buddha nature so that you consciously emanate in a new physical form out of your love and compassion for all beings. This completes a full cycle of the true nature's rhythm: day becomes twilight and night, followed by dawn and the sunshine of another day. Then we can have breakfast, but not only that, we get to have a birthday party!

This is just a brief introduction to the process of death and dying and living according to the teachings of Buddha Shakyamuni and Guru Padmasambhava. Again, the most important time for us is this life—where we are right now. We should try to do good things connected with unconditional love, compassion, and wisdom. When we do these positive activities, we should try to be in touch with our true nature and not get caught up in too much grasping or clinging. That is the best preparation for the next stages that we'll go through. This is what the teachings often say. The present time is very crucial and important for us—it is in our hands, under our control, and we can do whatever we want. This is where we can make positive changes that will greatly support our future destinations and activities.

Of course, in our lives we have so many important things to do. But our activities of true love, compassion, and wisdom are so special and rewarding. Even the smallest expression of love and compassion contributes to a much larger vision in ways that are so special, we can't even imagine. Therefore, we shouldn't ignore even the smallest positive action. It really benefits ourselves and everyone, and we're setting a very beautiful foundation that will grow and provide positive support for everyone as we go through the natural changes of life and death. This is what the teachings say, and this is how we can beautifully use our time now to prepare for the next bardos of death and dying.

Lineage of the Bardo Teachings

*B*ardo is a Tibetan word. *Bar* means "between," and *do* signifies "place" or "island," so it can be translated as "in-between place" or "intermediate state." The term *bardo* is used to describe the primary transitions through the various levels of experience that constitute the process of embodiment and reincarnation. Bardo teachings are about the continuity and ongoing nature of mind and experience. These instructions relate directly to everyday life as well as to death. If we can recognize what is happening right here, while we're alive, we can go forward with confidence.

According to the Buddha, all sentient beings are naturally enlightened and have been pure since the beginning. However, due to a small mistake, a little grasping develops into ego-clinging and a cyclic state of delusion. As long as we're deluded, awareness of our true nature is obscured. The bardo is the interval from the beginning of delusion until we return to our primordial nature. All our wandering in between is the bardo. Until we reach enlightenment, everything we feel, know, and experience is bardo phenomena. Even now we are wandering in an intermediate state. This will continue as long as we persist in clinging to the dualistic belief in the inherent existence of the self and the world.

The bardos don't exist outside of us. They are the context of our experience. This is very important to understand. Don't think that you are only in the bardo at certain times. The entire universe of samsara and nirvana happens within the bardos. From the onset of our dreams until we completely wake up to become enlightened is all bardo territory. As long as we are trapped by ego-clinging and attachment, we're in the bardo. Even highly realized beings and great practitioners arise within this process, but they are already awake so they don't make false distinctions between the bardo and pristine awareness. They understand that everything that appears is a display of primordial wisdom.

The bardo teachings came from Buddha Shakyamuni, who lived in the fifth and sixth centuries BCE, and continued through Guru Padmasambhava, who brought them to Tibet in the eighth century CE. Guru Padmasambhava's instructions and explanations regarding the bardo are very specific and clear, while Buddha Shakyamuni's are more general and are spread throughout his discourses. When Guru Padmasambhava came to Tibet, he gave some bardo teachings to his students, and with the help of the wisdom dakini Yeshe Tsogyal he hid other teachings in different areas to be discovered in the future.* Over the generations, many great *tertons*, or treasure revealers, have brought them forth, with the result that there are now extensive teachings on the bardos.

To awaken sentient beings of various capacities, Buddha Shakyamuni offered many levels of instruction that have been categorized into nine *yanas*, or levels of study and practice. The cycle of teachings known as the Zhitro, which refers to the peaceful and wrathful deities† that manifest following the dissolution of the body while in the bardo state, is

---

*A dakini (Tibetan *khandro*) is a female body of enlightenment who can take a human form or a meditational form that represents the enlightened state.
†In Tibetan Buddhism, a "deity" or "deities" represent the different aspects of our own inherently enlightened mind. In Western esotericism, which is also nondualistic, "deity" similarly represents the different aspects of the one God. In Tibetan Buddhism, all deities, or *yidams*, are also enlightened buddhas—fully awakened beings who manifest in different ways depending on what's helpful to uproot suffering and achieve happiness for all beings.

Buddha Shakyamuni, the historical Buddha
Padma Samye Ling gonpa murals

considered part of the inner tantras,* which are the esoteric teachings of the Buddha. It is a condensed teaching based on the essential meaning of the Guhyagarbha Tantra, a foundational text of Nyingma Buddhism, whose twenty-two chapters outline the path to enlightenment. Many great masters have said that the Zhitro teachings are the "inner tantra of the inner tantras." In this case we're not making distinctions among the

---

*The esoteric tantric teachings of the Buddha are dividied into outer and inner aspects. The outer tantras empower us to fully connect to and embody our buddha nature by emphasizing outer supports like body postures, purification practices, and rituals. The inner tantras enable one to fully recognize and manifest one's enlightened nature instantaneously, and from that realization, outer expressions like ritual become expressions of one's enlightened activity.

Guru Padmasambhava, known affectionately as Guru Rinpoche, "Precious Guru"

Padma Samye Ling gonpa murals

various inner tantras, nor between the creation and completion stages,* but joining them all together. This is the union of *rigpa*, or enlightened mind, and emptiness, the oneness of birth, death, and life experiences. There is no basis for discriminating because all are aspects of the one true nature. Nothing is rejected or exclusively accepted. This teaching is known as the one that unifies everything into a single state.

Guru Padmasambhava transmitted the bardo teachings to many students in Tibet, all of whom achieved enlightenment. Historically, many of these masters were Dzogchen adepts, and that view is central to the Zhitro teachings. Bardo instructions were spread through both the long oral tradition of *kama*, the oral teachings of the Buddha, as well as

---

*The creation stage approach emphasizes the more tangible aspects of pure body and pure speech, or "deity" and "mantra," while the completion stage highlights formless pure mind, or dharmakaya. The creation stage gradually brings these three aspects of pure body, speech, and mind together as a developmental sequence, while the completion stage emphasizes that they are already naturally united.

the short, direct lineage of *terma*, the mind treasures concealed by Guru Padmasambhava to be revealed when the timing is correct.

The hidden terma teachings of Guru Padmasambhava became very popular through tertons such as Karma Lingpa in the fourteenth century. One of the great masters, he discovered the Zhitro treasure known as *Zabcho Zhitro Gongpa Rangdrol*, "Self-Liberated Profound Realization of the Peaceful and Wrathful Ones," a part of which contains the Bardo Thodrol, which has been translated into English as "The Tibetan Book of the Dead."

Traditionally, there are five great tertons: Dorje Lingpa, Ratna Lingpa, Padma Lingpa, Karma Lingpa, and Sangye Lingpa, each of whom is related to the five directions: respectively, the east, south, west, north, and center. Karma Lingpa was a reincarnation of one of the twenty-five students of Guru Padmasambhava known as Chokro

Karma Lingpa
Padma Samye Ling gonpa murals

The five great tertons, or treasure revealers: Dorje Lingpa (top), Ratna Lingpa (right), Pema Lingpa (bottom), Karma Lingpa (left), and Sangye Lingpa (center)

Padma Samye Ling gonpa murals

Lui Gyaltsen, a famous translator of the Kangyur (the words of the Buddha as translated into Tibetan) in ninth-century Tibet. Many of the Buddha's Vinaya teachings, the code of discipline for monks and nuns, were rendered into Tibetan by this master. After receiving instructions from Guru Padmasambhava, eighth-century scholar Shantarakshita, and ninth-century scholar Vimalamitra, he practiced and became enlightened. Through his bodhichitta commitment and the wishes of Guru Padmasambhava, Chokro Lui Gyaltsen reincarnated many times in Tibet as various tertons and great bodhisattvas. One of those reincarnations who lived in the fourteenth century was a lay practitioner named Karma Lingpa.

Karma Lingpa, the "northern" terton, was born in southeastern Tibet. Following Guru Padmasambhava's instructions, he discovered the Zhitro teachings and other concealed treasures on Mount Gampodar in southeast Tibet, where the rock formations resemble dancing gods. After extracting the termas, he practiced them in complete secrecy as requested by Guru Padmasambhava. He only shared them years later

Chokro Lui
Gyaltsen

Padma Samye Ling
gonpa murals

with his son, Nyida Choje. Both Karma Lingpa and Nyida Choje practiced the Zhitro in secret and upon death acquired rainbow bodies.* For three generations, these instructions were transmitted to only a single person. Finally, in the nineteenth century, the grandson of Karma Lingpa, Gyarawa Namkha Chokyi Gyamtso, received the Zhitro transmission. Gyarawa Namkha Chokyi Gyamtso presented this teaching just three times during his entire life. Since then, this cycle of teachings has been among the most popular in Tibetan Buddhism and is still practiced every day by many high-level practitioners, renowned lamas, and monastic and lay meditators. Entire families will recite it early in the morning. Even those who don't know how to read learn to memorize it from hearing other members of the family chant it daily.

The Zhitro does not just cover the bardos after we die. It is a complete teaching that covers birth and living as well as dying and death and

---

*In some enlightened beings who have died, the body becomes smaller and smaller as it dissolves, emanating rainbow light, and finally only the hair and nails are left behind.

what follows death. The Tibetan Book of the Dead is just a small part of the Zhitro. The full Zhitro text is huge and contains detailed explanations of the visualization and completion stages, Dzogchen teachings and practices designed to remove mental obscurations and realize the clear light. It is an entire cycle, but only the bardo section has been translated recently.* The rendering of these teachings in the Tibetan language is especially beautiful. Each of Guru Padmasambhava's words has special mantric power, revealing the inner meaning of many visions and experiences.

The bardo instructions provide us with a body of techniques and practices that we can use to discover our buddha nature. If we are well-acquainted with the bardos we won't be surprised or confused when major transitions take place during our lives or between lives. Instead, we'll enjoy a continuity of understanding and spiritual growth. Of course, to develop such a panoramic view takes courage, confidence, and commitment.

In the terma discovered by Karma Lingpa, Guru Padmasambhava introduces six different bardos. The first bardo begins when we take birth and continues as long as we're alive. The second is the bardo of dreaming. The third is the bardo of concentration or meditation. The fourth occurs at the moment of death. The fifth is known as the "bardo of the luminosity of the true nature." The sixth is called the "bardo of transmigration" or "karmic becoming." This is the six-fold division of the bardos. Now we will go into a little more detail on each of them.

- The first bardo of birth and life lasts from the time you are conceived in your mother's womb until your last breath, when your consciousness leaves the body at death. In Tibetan this is called the *chenay*, the "tranquility bardo."
- The second is the *milam*, or "dream bardo." In other teachings this is considered a subdivision of the first bardo because sleeping and dreaming are regular aspects of our everyday lives. There are ways

---

*Gyurme Dorje (1950–2020) was a Scottish Tibetologist who translated the entire Bardo Thodrol in 2005.

to learn to integrate the dream state into our practice so that even while sleeping we can develop our realization.

- The third is the *samten*, the "perfection of meditation bardo." Generally, this is only experienced by meditators and those who are looking for inner peace and understanding. The onset and duration of this bardo depends on the capability of the practitioner. This meditation bardo is also considered a subdivision of the bardo of birth and living. Guru Padmasambhava categorized them this way because dreams and meditation are very important aspects of life and practice. Meditation is the primary method of maturing our spiritual insight and understanding. It allows us to go beyond the confusion of the bardo into the clarity of the primordial nature.

- The fourth is the *chikai*, or "bardo of dying," the moment of death. It begins when the outer and inner signs indicate that death is approaching and continues through the dissolution of the elements until the moment after the last breath, or perhaps a few minutes after the expiration of the last breath, when the inner breath has completely stopped.

- The fifth is the *chonyid*, the "luminosity of the true nature bardo," also known as the *dharmata*, which begins right after the last breath. In the outer sense this is commonly considered the moment of death; however, inwardly there is still a subtle movement of winds that continue to dissolve in stages. At this point, sounds and lights appear to burst forth with tremendous power. In the Dzogchen teachings these are said to arise spontaneously without anyone calling them up. Along with these visions, there's an experience of profound peace and pristine awareness, which could continue anywhere from one second to half an hour or more.

- The sixth bardo, or *sidpa*, is the "bardo of becoming," or transmigration. Ordinary beings who have never practiced and have failed to recognize the clear light at the moment of death are usually confused or distracted throughout the fifth bardo of luminosity. Eventually they arrive in the sixth bardo, the final stage before rebirth. This phase lasts until we have visions of our new parents and are conceived in a womb. The average duration of the period

The wheel of samsara

Padma Samye Ling gonpa murals

between death and rebirth is forty-nine days, although it could be as short as three. It's not always the same for everyone. Under certain conditions it could be a lot longer, but on average it lasts for forty-nine days.

The bardo process mirrors the wheel of dependent origination, a key Buddhist doctrine that says that everything that exists is dependent on something else, be it the universe, individuals, or thoughts and objects; in other words, it refers to interdependence, which turns on and on, so that after we die and transmigrate through the bardos we again take birth and live. This cycle continues until we are totally enlightened.

The purpose of studying the bardo sequence is not simply to have a general familiarity with these states, but to become skilled in recognizing them. Using these teachings wisely will allow us to develop our realization and will provide invaluable skillful means to benefit all beings.

Because of their supreme importance, Guru Padmasambhava gave extensive instructions on the bardos. Since we are all travelers on this highway, we should be aware of our circumstances and make good use of these teachings.

First Bardo of Birth and Life

We will now begin a detailed discussion of each of the six bardos following the line-by-line commentary on *The Root Prayer of the Six Bardos*, which is part of a larger terma text revealed by Karma Lingpa whose translated title is "Self-Liberated Profound Realization of the Peaceful and Wrathful Ones." Our commentary is also based on an additional terma text known as *Narak Tongtruk*, "Shaking the Depths of the Lower Realms," which was revealed in the seventeenth century by the great terton Tsasum Lingpa. *Narak Tongtruk* is part of Tsasum Lingpa's larger terma cycle known as *Kagyad Chenmo Sangwa Zilnon*, "Dominating Secret Power of the Great Eight Herukas."

The bardo of birth and life refers to the present time and experience. We have already taken birth and are still alive, so we are now in the first bardo. How should we use this time in a meaningful way? Guru Padmasambhava made it clear that to take advantage of this opportunity and fulfill our aspirations during this life, we have to learn to focus our mind, since our time here isn't going to last forever.

> *When the birthplace bardo is dawning upon me,*
> *There is no spare time in this life; abandoning laziness . . .**

---

*In most cases, direct quotations from the root text and related commentaries have been indented and set off as seen here.

We can never be sure how long we will be in the bardo of living. No one can say. When and where we will die is always uncertain. It is completely unpredictable. No matter how rich or clever you are, you can never know how much longer you have to live. Since we're not sure how long this life will last, Guru Padmasambhava advises us to abandon laziness. Now is the time to increase appreciation and gratitude for our life situation, to arouse ourselves and make a joyful effort in order to realize great results. We should develop confidence and be happy in our endeavors. Don't just assume that you're worthless and incapable. Don't let this opportunity slip away and be a cause for regret. Learn to work effectively, happily, and with firm commitment. The biggest obstacle to spiritual progress is laziness. There are many forms of laziness, but they all share the feeling that there is plenty of time. "I won't bother with this today. I'll do it later." When we think like this again and again, we miss many important opportunities and lose sight of our goal. That is the worst thing about laziness.

Another type of laziness is based on doubt: "How could *I* ever do this?" You put yourself down and even feel special in considering yourself so low and incapable. To overcome this requires courage. Discover your natural dignity. Feel the preciousness of this moment, how amazing it is to be alive! If you understand the truth of this, there's nothing you can't accomplish. That's exactly what the Buddha and many other great masters did. They worked on the basis of this inspiration. Since we all have buddha nature and inherent wisdom, why can't we do as they did? We need to apply ourselves diligently and engage in our practice fearlessly.

Yet another type of laziness has to do with attaching to lesser interests and missing the greater opportunity. You know that the practice is special, you have some awareness that this is a very unique moment, and you are inspired by this beautiful opening, but you still waste time and cling to meaningless worldly involvements. You're like a cat who is always trying to catch another mouse. Guru Padmasambhava taught that this kind of activity is as endless as waves on the ocean. Just when you think you're going to finish, the next wave arrives, and then another. There is always something else to do or acquire. This form of laziness involves staying distracted with countless things to achieve and do. There will never come a time when we've completed everything. These preoccupations never cease. Unaware of the cause of this unsettledness, we habitually cling to external things and are subject to an endless procession of wandering thoughts and impulsive actions. This happens all the time when we're attached to external things. If we start looking inward we will discover the source of all these restless feelings. We will also find joy, tranquility, and thoughts that bring peace and harmony.

Don't believe this just because Guru Padmasambhava said it. Look into the history of renowned people, warriors, kings, or those with great artistic talent. All of them died with dreams and projects unfulfilled. Everyone leaves this world with unfinished business. Investigate this for yourself. You'll find that this is really true.

When we see laziness in ourselves, what should we do? Respond immediately and with vigor. Don't fall for "I'll do it later." You don't have to be patient with laziness. Guru Padmasambhava said that when you observe laziness in yourself, act like a timid person who has just discovered that a snake has crawled up into your lap. You would not just sit there to see what the snake does next. You'd get right up, throw it off, and run away. Guru Padmasambhava also said that to overcome laziness you must act immediately, like someone whose hair has just caught on fire. These are very clear examples about how to respond to laziness.

Among the six bardos, the first bardo of birth and living is the most important one we have to learn about. This is where we can really develop, grow strong, realize what is precious, and fully awaken to our buddha nature so that we can easily handle the remaining bardos. Through practice and meditation we can learn to recognize our true nature and move through all the changes of birth and death with great confidence and joy. We won't have to worry, be concerned, or even hesitate. Everything we need will appear in the palm of our hand; we'll be right on track.

Guru Padmasambhava said that if we practice well during this bardo we can transmigrate without doubts, returning home like a hawk who makes a safe nest high on a cliffside. She easily flies up and enters her nest without any hesitation or indecision. If we absorb the meaning of these teachings in our hearts during this life, the rest of the bardos will not cause us any concern. We will move through them with confidence and full awareness so that they all become part of the glorious adventure. Guru Padmasambhava emphasizes just how precious this time is, right where we are now. Refrain from nonvirtuous actions. Constantly be engaged in activities that will bring benefit to ourselves and other beings. Many teachings state that where we are now is an island of jewels: we can find all kinds of valuable gems here in the form of opportunities to awaken to our true nature. We must take some in our hands, put some in our pockets, and fill our backpack. If we return empty-handed, the cycle of samsara revolves again.

Time does not wait for us. We should use it to do something meaningful. Of course there are many things we have to do just to get along in this world, but as much as we can we should really expand our view and adjust our attitude. Guru Padmasambhava advises us to be attentive to the present but not to neglect looking toward the future, to think about tomorrow as well as the next day, next year, and the following years, too. If we think in this way, gradually we will develop the intelligence and compassion necessary to actualize benefits for all living beings, today, tomorrow, and continually.

These teachings were given by Guru Padmasambhava himself. The same truth has been spoken by all the buddhas and bodhisattvas. All of the great masters who have benefited beings for generations worked hard to develop love, compassion, and bodhichitta. That's the standard they kept. We should do the same. Think of the men and women who became spiritual masters, and keep them close in mind. Learn to do as they did. We should not deceive ourselves. We might think we're very smart, but if we're still fooling around, the cycle of karmic bondage will remain intact.

Abandoning laziness,
Enter undistractedly in the three paths of
Listening, reflection, and meditation.

Guru Padmasambhava and Buddha Shakyamuni both said that we should do three things: study, contemplate, and meditate. At first, study and consider the teachings, then contemplate them. To settle the mind we must first become aware of the obstacles and obscurations that are masking its true nature. Finally we are ready to meditate.

Meditation is the fruit of study and contemplation. In this context, meditation doesn't mean merely sitting calmly and focusing the mind on an external object; here we are resting our mind in its true nature. Since the true nature pervades everything both internally and externally, meditating on it clarifies our view and helps us to fully understand both subjective and objective phenomena. The focus in meditation should be on the nature of the mind itself. This will reveal everything.

Meditation on the true nature yields a lucidity and profound openness that is very mysterious. Abiding continuously in that state will cause beautiful qualities like compassion and wisdom to arise and shine naturally. At first, thoughts will become less interesting or insistent. As you learn to abide in deep meditation for longer periods, dualistic conceptions will be completely pacified. When you become freely established in the radiance of the primordial nature, thoughts will become like servants. At that point you will have a greater capacity to take responsibility for your mental events.

Gradually, a great blissfulness will arise. At that point there will be no more suffering, only an unshakable equanimity as you merge with the true nature. Once you gain authority over conceptions and the mind, you become more capable of mastering all the other aspects of your life. Every moment becomes workable because you understand the bardo process.

Listening, contemplating, and meditating are known as "the three wisdoms." Each of these practices is vital to actualizing our buddha nature and our ability to benefit others. First, listen carefully and closely to the teachings you receive.* This should encourage and inspire you to make a joyful effort. Do not simply collect teachings—look into

---

*"Listening" could be either hearing words with your ears or reading words in a book such as this one.

their implications and contemplate their meaning. Then, apply them to yourself so that what you've received does not merely penetrate your ears and brain. Really connect with the meaning behind the instructions, take them into your heart, and reaffirm the truth of each word with your own understanding. This is contemplation. By deeply contemplating the teachings, you will naturally actualize the result, which is meditation. Meditation will help mature what you've learned so that your knowledge is not simply intellectual or conceptual. Results will ripen as you grow. Although all three are indispensable, meditation is the most important.

To apply these three practices, we must learn to recognize and release the tendency to indulge in distractions. This is especially true when we are just beginning, but distractions can be a serious hindrance at every stage of practice, especially during meditation. The Dzogchen teachings say, "There is no meditation. Nondistraction is the meditation." The Prajnaparamita, or "Perfection of Wisdom" teachings by the Buddha, extensively discuss the many ways that duality mind mistakenly fixates on various distractions, preventing our buddha nature from recognizing the interdependent, empty nature of everything, which is known as Prajnaparamita.*

Distractions come uninvited, so we need a clear, vivid mindfulness to undermine their influence and to practice effectively. This doesn't always come easily, even if we have the right motivation and can sustain a joyful effort. Learn to listen undistractedly. Do not let your attention wander during contemplation practice. Avoid clinging to ideas and images while in meditation. To avoid following thoughts, be mindful and observe with relaxed alertness.

The next line in the prayer explains the result, actualized through the practice of the three wisdoms:

---

*In the Perfection of Wisdom teachings, Buddha Shakyamuni listed ten types of distractions that can occur during practice and prevent our progress: (1) nonexistent nature, (2) existent nature, (3) exaggeration, (4) deprecation, (5) the conception of one, (6) the conception of many, (7) identity, (8) discrimination, (9) holding titles and names, and (10) conceptions of meaning.

> *Bringing appearance and thoughts to the path,*
> *Realize the nature of the three kayas.*

Actualization of the three kayas, or "bodies" or "dimensions," is the result of applying the three wisdoms. The kayas represent three inseparable aspects of the Buddha: the dharmakaya, the sambhogakaya, and the nirmanakaya.* Yet according to the inner tantras, the three kayas have no objective existence. They are not localized, but are all-pervasive, encompassing both mind and appearances. This means that everything is always in a state of perfect enlightenment.

All phenomena are a display of the three kayas, or *trikaya*. The three kayas are never separate from one another, but exist primordially within the true nature. The trikaya is what we and all external phenomena essentially are. When you fully realize what you are, you will know that you never had to do anything or go anywhere in order to be enlightened or see a pureland. The purelands *are* the trikaya, and all six bardos arise within these kayas. The display, activity, and true nature of the kayas are all within us. It's not a matter of escaping from "this horrible place" to somewhere else that is fancy and beautiful, where the three kayas dwell. We must realize the three kayas as the true nature and reality of *all* phenomena.

Infinite and uncreated, the true nature of mind is great emptiness— the inconceivable openness known as the *dharmakaya*. Great emptiness is not blank, empty space, a void, or nothingness. It is very luminous, clear, and full. Brightness and clarity shine forth spontaneously. The quality of unceasing luminosity of the true nature is known as the *sambhogakaya*. The mind is always active, radiating a world of transformations. Due to its natural responsiveness it never stays the same for

---

*The three kayas represent three inseperable aspects of the true nature. The *dharmakaya* is the formless absolute nature, beyond concepts, or the "truth body" from which all forms manifest; it represents the absolute. The *nirmanakaya* is the more tangible, outreaching form body, or relative aspect. The *sambhogakaya* is the semiform light body that is intermediary between these two and is that which experiences the bliss of enlightenment. Or put another way, the dharmakaya is sometimes compared to the sky, the sambhogakaya is the clouds, and the nirmanakaya is the rain. Please see the glossary for additional details.

two instants. Each sparkling, radiant moment of manifest existence is never separate from the original state of the true nature. Each spark is the union of emptiness and clarity. That radiance, when manifesting as momentary events in space and time, is known as the *nirmanakaya*.

Guru Padmasambhava taught that the three kayas are inherent in the nature of mind. Many people don't know this and are always wandering, looking for something outside of themselves. This search opens them to many experiences: good and bad, high and low, deep and shallow, and sequences of gain and loss. But in every case these experiences are concepts that are created by the mind. None of these qualities exist in a solid, objective sense. The present flows and changes, and this impermanence indicates that there is no inherent existence in objects and events.

All perceptions and conscious experience are nothing other than the expression of our minds. Everything we see, hear, feel, taste, smell, and touch is mind. What does mind really refer to? Mind is open, empty, and pure from the beginning. Mind is also the embodiment of the three kayas. Our practice is to discover and express the true nature of the mind. We must study, contemplate, meditate on, and ultimately actualize the trikaya realization. If we are devoted and one-pointed in our efforts, all phenomena will reveal the trikaya. When the moment of death comes we will recognize this event as a lucid display of the three kayas—another expression of the true nature. There is no conflict when we understand that this is part of a natural process.

The bardo of birth and life is a very special circumstance for practice. Since everything is pervaded by the three kayas, we must recognize that our present vision and perception are ultimately not any different from the original nature of the mind. The understanding of the innate purity of all perception is the highest teaching of the inner tantras. All of our dualistic conceptions such as self and other, good and bad, assisting friends and avoiding enemies arise as thoughts in our minds. Mind creates all of these fabrications. There's nothing in all of those names that has any solid existence, yet the mind creates notions and projects visions that we are inclined to believe and act on. Distracted and unmindful, we habitually grasp and cling.

What is grasping? To grasp means to be attached to what we think. It is to believe that things actually exist the way the conditioned mind perceives them. We continually cling to beliefs and create artificial divisions. We've decided that some things are good and others are not. This clinging to concepts is based on the assumption of permanence. Even though phenomena are constantly changing, the mind projects a fixed image and holds on to it, assuming things are a certain way all the time. Trying to see the world as we'd like it to be and holding on to that image is ego-clinging. It's like we're suffocating in a tight cocoon. Trapped by attachments, we miss opportunities to release our grasping and grow.

Being confined to a small room with no space to move back and forth creates a contraction in the body. When we want to shift our position, there is no room, so we suffer. We move a little to one side, but it's still uncomfortable. We suffer at every turn because our movements are constricted. This is the effect that ego-clinging and grasping have on both body and mind. We create a small, cramped space for ourselves and others by withholding love and compassion. Ego-clinging, grasping, and dualistic thinking make us narrow and uptight so that we automatically communicate these qualities to others. They tend to make everybody uncomfortable.

Actually, the door in the room is wide open. But if we don't walk through it, it may as well be sealed. We suffer because we're convinced of our limitations. Yet when we open our hearts and minds and love all beings equally, we are liberated into the infinite expanse, the reality beyond all limits, the original, primordial nature of our mind, which is forever open and free. By releasing ego-clinging, we are merely returning to our primordial nature as it already is, as it always has been.

By cherishing dualistic notions such as absolute good and evil, we subconsciously develop hopes and fears that lead to emotional cycles of elation and depression. We push away what we don't like and assume that there's something good we should cling to and expect. If these assumptions go unchallenged, hope and fear can destroy our vision and crush us. We lose our power and true identity under their influence.

Where do hopes and fears come from? They originate in the mind when it grasps dualistic concepts. Mind is the principal source of everything. But where is the mind? As we begin to search for an answer, we should know that we're not going to find any solid, substantially existent mind. Everything disappears as fast as it arises. The deeper we look, the more it disappears, until we come to the point where we can't find anything at all. At that point the search is complete. We really will have no idea what to do next! In one sense we are completely lost. In another, we're quickly approaching the primordial state that the Buddha called "great emptiness." Here there are no fixed divisions, distinctions, or boundaries. We've reached the ultimate point: the original, infinite, true nature of the mind. By diligently chasing rainbows, we finally reach a horizon where there is no longer anything to pursue. Everything merges in that unfathomable state. As the mind dissolves in the boundless dimension of the true nature, relax and remain in meditation. This is the central place. When there is no disturbance or dualism of body and mind, that is real meditation. It doesn't require any magic. Simply observe your own mind. If you keep looking into it, you'll eventually realize the bliss of perfect equanimity.

The practice of meditation teaches us to transcend the conceptual distinctions between appearances and thoughts. Subject and object fuse into a single awareness. We no longer see a world of inherently existent entities. In reality, even atoms are not actually solid. Although they exhibit many properties, they're not concrete, independent objects. Every apparent thing is an impermanent mental construct based on the interdependence of everything. Nothing exists outside of this interdependence. There are many subatomic particles in even the smallest atom.

Every entity is composed of parts, and each part is made up of even smaller parts, and this continues on down to infinity. Atoms and everything they constitute are nothing but the mysterious lighting up of the true nature as appearances. This is why great masters can walk in the sky or transform the elements. You could say they aren't really changing anything when they do these things; they're actually demonstrating the interdependent reality and true nature of arising phenomena.

The primordial nature is wonderfully inconceivable. Void of inherent existence, great emptiness is perfectly open and flexible. Each and every luminous manifestation is precious and unique. We can see this in many ways. For instance, all beings have slightly different perceptual systems. Animals, gods, and human beings experience very different worlds. But this is true even among humans from the same culture.

Look at this. [Khenchen Rinpoche holds up a bell.] Although everyone can name this, we each have our own way of perceiving and understanding what it is. The way you see the color red is not the way everyone sees it. Things do not inherently exist the way they appear. The mind has a very special way of speaking to each of us, because different beings can look at a single object and not see the same thing. This is very unique! Obvious discrepancies such as the difference in our points of view are part of the relativity of the external world. But inwardly it goes deeper than this. We all have different approaches and make unique associations that support our particular way, so that each of us sees a personal version of the world. This is the reason why there are so many different buddhas. For example, the Five Dhyani Buddhas* each realized their buddha nature in a slightly different way and then displayed their special qualities for the benefit of all beings.

Like athletes who train for the Olympics to win a gold medal, the bardo of birth and life is the training ground to exercise and actualize our skills so that the other bardos—particularly the fourth, fifth, and sixth bardos of dying, after death, and becoming—provide the conditions to acquire a gold, silver, or bronze medal. The first bardo is the best place to develop these valuable skills. Emphasizing this point, the text reads,

At this moment,
Where we have for once attained a human body . . .

It is very special and precious to be human, to be surrounded by all this wealth and beauty, and to have the opportunity to realize buddhahood. This is a very crucial time. Don't take this for granted and

---

*The Five Dhyani Buddhas represent five aspects of enlightened awareness that unlike the historical buddha, Gautama Siddhartha, represent subtle qualities and transcendent states of wisdom mind. In addition, they are five living buddhas who constantly support all beings to achieve awakening.

waste it. Actualize your true nature. The human realm is a unique place where we can work to accomplish something meaningful and develop our understanding. Buddha Shakyamuni reiterated this many times throughout his life. As we can see by observing what goes on in this world, it is not a pureland, but it's the best place for us to learn and develop ourselves. There are many other worlds—some are exceptionally beautiful, luxurious, and comfortable. In comparison, ours might not look that wonderful, but it's actually a very special place. Here we can mature spiritually and transcend our limitations. There is a lot here that challenges us to grow, helping us to discover and express our buddha nature. Qualities such as courage, confidence, and love are called forth in response to many situations. If we accomplish something meaningful here, we will be able to go to other places and enjoy higher realizations. But for now this is the place where we must do something significant with our lives.

By practicing during the bardo of birth and life, great meditators can become enlightened within one lifetime. Yogis and yoginis with high realization are able to perceive the entire universe as the mandala of the deities, so that every form is seen as a buddha's body and environment, all sounds are perceived as the pure speech or mantra of enlightened beings, and every thought and emotion is experienced as the wisdom mind of the buddhas. Recognizing the true nature of this continually unfolding vision is part of the spontaneous activity of pristine cognition. Ultimately, everything appears as a display of primordial wisdom, and within that realization we can begin to help all sentient beings. As Guru Padmasambhava said, "It is not the time to continue fooling around."

Second Bardo of the Dream State

If you have a deep understanding of the bardo of birth and life, you can also learn to make good use of the time you spend dreaming. In Tibetan this is called the *milam* bardo.

According to the Vajrayana teachings, the bardo of birth and life can be divided into two basic categories: the experience of the day and the experience of the night. During daytime we work and are physically active. At night we lie down, relax, and then sleep becomes our major occupation. Animals have similar habit patterns.

Each day we go out and engage in many activities with our body, speech, and mind. Normally, people aren't trying to cultivate positive qualities and accumulate merit. Most of the time we're bound up with feelings like jealousy and competitiveness, which are based on ignorance and attachment. These are typical emotions that characterize human beings during the day.

At night, most people go to sleep. While asleep, habit patterns similar to those experienced during the day recycle through our minds, so our dreams follow the pattern of activity that was established during the day. If you tend to be competitive or dramatize emotions such as desire or anger, those same qualities will also arise in dreams and condition your experience until morning.

Sleep is a very important part of our lives. Like nutrition, it's necessary for our physical well-being. While we sleep, our body and speech are not doing anything—all external activities cease. Our five senses become inactive: the eyes don't see, the ears don't hear, the nose doesn't smell, the tongue doesn't taste, and the body doesn't feel. At various places in the Buddha's teachings, sleep is described as a state of dullness. It's also known as the "little death." All five consciousnesses merge into the sixth consciousness of dualistic thinking. This is where dreams occur. The mind consciousness wanders through our channels under the influence of habitual tendencies, and we begin dreaming.

In the dream state, everything you see is a reflection of your habit patterns. You might be falling from the top of a two-hundred-story building or be flying through the sky without a plane. You may suddenly find yourself desperately trying to escape your captors, or lazing around in the lap of fantastic luxury. Perhaps you've won the lottery, or conversely, you're distressed over losing a million dollars. Whatever you experience is not happening anywhere except in the space above your pillow. Everything you encounter in the dream bardo arises entirely within the domain of your tiny consciousness and its habit patterns.

Most of the dreaming we do at night reflects the actions and attitudes of the daytime: accepting and rejecting, analyzing, arguing, and fighting—all kinds of emotions and activities occur, just as they do in our waking experience. Our mind is carried by the emotions according to habit patterns, whether we're awake or asleep. Most dreams—perhaps 80 percent—are related to conditioning acquired in this lifetime. About 20 percent are connected to past lifetimes or relate to something that has not yet happened but because it potentially exists, our mind reflects it through dreams. About 2 or 3 percent relate to our spiritual path, such as encounters with buddhas and bodhisattvas. These dreams strengthen our motivation and encourage the practice of pure love and compassion. But no matter what type of dream it is, all dreams are experiences communicated by the mind to the mind, so that even in sleep, our mind is busy.

The second stanza says:

> *When the dream bardo is dawning upon me,*
> *Abandoning carelessly and stupidly lying like a corpse . . .*

Since we spend a lot of our lives sleeping, Guru Padmasambhava uses strong words like these to arouse and awaken us to the importance of developing a continuity of mindfulness and clarity in the dream state. If we live for a hundred years, almost forty of them are spent sleeping. If we can use this time for practice, we can significantly increase the time we have to actualize a meaningful result. The Vajrayana dream yoga teachings provide us with an extremely skillful method to expand the practice of mindfulness into the dream state, so that we don't just sleep in an ordinary, wasteful way.

The third line clearly explains how we should sleep:

> *Enter in the natural sphere of unwavering attentiveness.*

Prepare for bed mindfully, keeping a pure motivation. Abandoning carelessness, try to fall asleep in a state of relaxed alertness. How do we practice mindfulness in the dream itself? This is explained in the fourth line:

> *Recognizing your dreams,*
> *Practice transforming illusion into luminosity.*

To make the time we spend dreaming more meaningful, we must first recognize that we are dreaming. This is the first exercise. The next step is called "transforming the dream." The third is known as "multiplying." The fourth practice is to unify the dream with clear light awareness. (1) Recognizing, (2) transforming, (3) multiplying, and (4) unifying the dream with the luminosity of the true nature—these are the four essential applications of dream yoga.

You can do these practices at any time, but normally you begin them before going to sleep at night. Start by aligning your motivation with bodhichitta and the awareness of natural purity. These two are the foundation and structure of the whole path. Without these, your practice will fall apart, even if you've already grown a little. Bodhichitta aspiration and awareness of purity are indispensable. Feel a deep love and compassion for all sentient beings, including yourself. Really open your heart to everyone. If you have any trouble with this, remember that you're doing this practice for all beings, and that everybody needs love in order to awaken their buddha nature. Think deeply about the many good reasons to generate compassion for everyone. Then work on applying it in the present moment by changing your attitude. Awareness of purity also means having a deep sense of appreciation and reverence toward all the buddhas, bodhisattvas, and lineage masters, as well as a good feeling about yourself and sincere gratitude for your life situation. All of this is really important. With this view and motivation, begin the dream yoga practice.

Relax your mind, letting go of all conceptions except those associated with bodhichitta. After a while even let go of these once you reach the sphere of the true nature, the infinite state. Relax as long as you can in the openness of the true nature, free of any mental fabrications or disturbances by mundane thoughts. Eliminate any trace of hope or fear, abandon analysis and discrimination, and let go of any emotions such as anger, jealousy, or attachment. Release everything—let it go in all directions and dissolve. Simply remain in the pristine awareness of the present moment.

Secondly, think, *Tonight, I'm definitely going to recognize the dream as a dream.* Develop a strong determination and encourage yourself to recognize any dreams you have while you sleep. Feel the supportive presence of the Buddha, Guru Padmasambhava, and the blessings of the bodhisattvas, who are all helping you to see the dream as a dream.

What we are at present, our sense of self, is already a type of dream. There's not really any way to make a fundamental distinction between our experience now and what we will dream tonight. Right now we are in a waking dream, and tonight we'll experience a sleeping dream. In this way, everything is a dream. Think about this deeply, because it's really true! Perceptions in the waking state are a reflection of your mind and mental events. This is also true of perceptions in dreams. So what is the difference between the waking state and the dream state? Consider the possibility that there is no basic difference. We're already in the dream state. At night, your dream self is lying in a dream bed, under dream blankets, in a dream house. All of these visions are dreams: the buddhas are dream beings, and our conceptions induce dreamlike states of day dreams and night dreams. They're all dreams. It is very important to contemplate this point thoroughly. Buddha Shakyamuni often told his disciples to regard all phenomena as dreams. He used many examples, like an echo, a city in the clouds, or a rainbow to illustrate the illusory nature of the phenomenal world. Dreams represent just one type of illusion. The whole universe arises and dissolves like a mirage. Everything about us, even the most enlightened qualities, are also dreamlike phenomena. There's nothing outside the dream of illusory being. So in going to sleep, you're just passing from one dream state to another.

With this understanding, lie down to sleep. Lie on your right side with your right hand underneath your right cheek. Keep your left leg on top of the right leg, with your left arm placed along the left side of your body. This is known as the lion's posture and was used by Buddha Shakyamuni as he prepared to enter mahaparinirvana.

First you must generate compassion and love for all dreamlike beings. Then combine this with an awareness of the essential purity of all things. The third step is to make a very strong resolution to

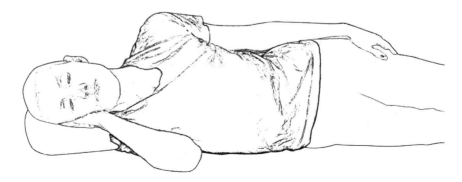

Lion's posture of dreaming
Drawing by Pema Dragpa

recognize that you're dreaming. Affirm your intention to realize that everything, including yourself, is a dream, and that what happens during sleep is only another dream. Intensify this determination and then concentrate. Various techniques may be used to support concentration, such as visualizing the bodies of the buddhas, seed syllables, or ritual objects.

One of the primary methods used to stabilize concentration during the transition from waking to sleeping is to visualize a red lotus in the speech center. Imagine a very fat red lotus with four petals that is in the process of blooming. The petals have not yet opened, but are not completely closed either. In the center of them is a bright red light. Concentrating on the light is sufficient. If you can manage another visualization, picture a small white triangle pointing downward at your third eye, inside of which sits a tiny Vajrasattva* who is usually visualized by himself.

As you lie there, focus on these forms. Let them become smaller and smaller, subtler and subtler; relax and let yourself go deeper and deeper. Then, the instant you think of it, Vajrasattva sends out a great white light from your third eye that covers your body. He then takes a seat in front of you. Go to sleep concentrating on that. Unless you've entered the *alaya*, the eighth consciousness or the ground of the mind, sooner or later you will begin to dream. If you're able to fall asleep without disturbing your concentration, you will easily be able to recognize that you're dreaming. Oftentimes when you recognize that you're dreaming you also wake up. Learn to maintain this recognition while continuing to sleep and dream.

Dream practice is important to do regularly with joyful effort. If we can recognize the dream as a dream, we can recognize the truth of any situation—even our own death. Often people don't recognize that they've died, but we'll say more about this when we get to the fifth bardo.

---

*Vajrasattva is a living Buddha as well as primordial esoteric form, beyond ego and illusory reality, who represents the perfect and complete embodiment of all the buddhas of the three times. Meditation and practice on Vajrasattva is a powerful support for purification, bringing clarity and peace of mind, increasing positive energy and auspicious conditions, and swiftly revealing our innate qualities of love, compassion, and wisdom.

Red lotus visualization

Line drawing by Andrea Nerozzi

Vajrasattva triangle visualization

Based on Padma Samye Ling gonpa murals

After you recognize the dream as a dream and can maintain that awareness without waking, continue to observe the dream. This prepares you for the second step in dream yoga, which is to transform the contents of the dream. Now you're going to play around and have some fun! This is where you can practice gymnastics. If you wish, you can free-fall from 37,000 feet and touch the earth and not get hurt before quickly jumping back up to your starting position!

In dreams you can transform anything, including yourself. If you want to be a lion, you'll immediately experience yourself as a lion and know how that feels. You can also be transformed into a mountain, a tree, the earth, water, a man or woman, a child, or any of the beings in the six realms. You're not bound by physical circumstances. You're free, independent, and can do whatever you like. There are no barriers— you can be anything. Go beyond the limits of your hopes and fears. For instance, we tend to distance ourselves from what we don't like, but in the dream we can creatively restructure phenomena, beings, and events to penetrate our fixed assumptions and remove our preconceptions, revealing the deeper truth beyond the boundaries and limitations

Five Dhyani Buddhas
Vajrakilaya and Medicine Buddha Temple, Padma Samye Ling

of dualistic systems and traditions. This is an exercise in openness and freedom, and is known as "transforming."

The third aspect of dream yoga is called "multiplying." Here, you're creating more opportunities and expanding qualities. In the transforming practice you change things, but only one thing at a time. Once you're good at this you can then multiply aspects of the dream numerous times. You might take a hundred forms or become ten different things at once. You could be various gods, a few buddhas, a naga, three bodhisattvas, a dozen human beings, many types of animals, and a grove of trees—all at the same time! You can multiply yourself in millions of forms. Increase the variety and open yourself to the way you embody the whole cosmic system. Understand that all of this is you. The inconceivable vastness of our nature is what is revealed by this practice.

If you accomplish this you can tour the purelands and visit all five of the Dhyani Buddhas at once, make offerings, receive teachings, and return from all five directions simultaneously. While you're meditating in the pureland of Ratnasambhava, listening to teachings and making offerings—even multiplying yourself and the offerings by thousands— you're also doing the same thing in the western pureland of Buddha Amitabha, as well as in the north in the presence of Amoghasiddhi, and in the center, where Buddha Vairochana turns the Wheel of Dharma in his pureland.

You can visit them one by one or be with them all and receive their teachings simultaneously. In the dream bardo, mind is faster than a space shuttle or even the speed of light. You can be anywhere in a moment. There are many different purelands where sentient beings can go to receive teachings and realize various benefits. This is really true.

All the great Nyingma tertons have gone to the pureland of Guru Padmasambhava in their dream state. Many of them also meet Guru Rinpoche and the wisdom dakini Yeshe Tsogyal face to face in the waking world, but this often happens in dreams, too. Typically, a terton returns from one of these dreams and writes a beautiful guidebook on the route he took, how he was received, who he contacted, and other details. Sometimes the vision includes a few weeks or a month's worth of experience, but in our time they inevitably return the very next morning.

For example, Tsasum Lingpa had a dream while he was camping on a mountain in central Tibet. He was just sleeping on the mountain without a tent or sleeping bag when four dakinis came and said, "Let's go now, you have to come." So he asked, "Where to?" "To see your parents," they replied as they held out a big shawl. "Sit here, we'll carry you." Tsasum Lingpa replied, "I don't want to go now. I'd rather stay here." But the dakinis told him, "You have to come. Now's the time, so let's go." They practically had to force him. Each dakini held a corner

Tsasum Lingpa

Drawing by Sergey Noskov

of the shawl and carried him off into the sky. As he flew over India, he looked down and wondered, *Which mountain is that? What is the name of that river?* His description is similar to what we experience when we travel by plane. Upon arrival, he had an audience with Yeshe Tsogyal and Guru Padmasambhava. Tsasum Lingpa mentioned that Yeshe Tsogyal was very kind to him. He attended a big ceremony with Guru Padmasambhava and many other realized beings. Yeshe Tsogyal had Tsasum Lingpa sit near her and this made him feel very happy. At

The dakini Yeshe Tsogyal, consort of Padmasambhava

Padma Samye Ling gonpa murals

the end, when they said he must return, he insisted that he didn't want to leave. Guru Padmasambhava told him that he should go now, but that he would be able to come back later.

He had already been there about three weeks when Yeshe Tsogyal walked him to the gate where the four dakinis awaited his return. She told him that she would never be apart from him, and after giving him more instructions, she said goodbye. When the dakinis dropped him off, he was back on the mountain, the sun was shining over his head, and he was sitting straight up. This type of vision was not unique to Tsasum Lingpa; many tertons have given similar accounts and details of what they saw in these purelands.

Another great eighteenth-century terton, Dudul Dorje, was also carried off into the sky by dakinis. When he arrived at Guru Padmasambhava's pureland he saw that it had four doors. His retinue approached and began to open the eastern gate when a great dakini appeared. She threw something in front of them that made everything go totally dark so they couldn't enter. Then the dakini guides led him to the southern gate. As it opened, the same great dakini appeared again and threw something black, which completely blocked the door. They went to the western and northern gates and the same thing happened. So Dudul Dorje asked the gatekeeper dakini, "Why are you so mean?" She said, "I'm not mean, but you were very cruel to me!" The terton replied, "I don't remember doing anything to you." So she explained, "We were both there when Jatson Nyingpo was giving teachings. I was the ugly old lady you were so mean to. Do you remember now? That's why I won't let you see Guru Padmasambhava." Dudul Dorje said, "Forgive me. I was wrong and apologize for my rudeness. I'm very sorry, that was inconsiderate of me." With that, she opened the gate wide.

These are just brief accounts, but many tertons have given elaborate descriptions of the purelands they have visited. For example, after the dakinis brought Tsasum Lingpa to the palace, they all opened the main gate together. He describes the color of the door and all of the things he saw when he walked in: beautiful gardens, an emanation of Guru Padmasambhava, some lamas, and many other specific details.

Every one of the great tertons kept thorough records of their experiences. If you're able to maintain awareness during the dream state you can do the same as these masters did. Visions like these will arise naturally. The great tertons don't actually have to do the dream yoga practices we're explaining here because they're always aware of the dreamlike nature of existence. Their ability to visit purelands reflects that understanding through the specific details of what they experience.

The fourth step is to unify the dream with clear light awareness—the luminosity aspect of the true nature. This is the most important of these exercises. Learn to maintain this understanding throughout the dream state. Whether you simply recognize the dream or go on to multiply and transform it, it is essential to maintain this unified awareness.

Clear light, or primordial luminosity, has many different aspects, but the most important is the complete absence of clinging and freedom from attachment. The best way to do dream yoga is to not cling to the dream, not be attached to recognizing the dream, not hold on to the results of multiplying or transforming, and in general to not cling to any of these practices. If you don't cling, dreams themselves take on a radiant, transformed quality, becoming almost transparent within clear light awareness. In this way, dreams become emanations of the five wisdoms. This is called "unifying the dream with the clear light," or "merging the dream with the luminosity of the true nature."

Don't sleep like an animal.
Do the practice which mixes sleep and reality.

In the fifth and sixth lines, Guru Padmasambhava is again encouraging us to develop the pure intention to become proficient in sustaining mindfulness and relaxed alertness in the bardo of dreaming. He is ushering us into the practice of mingling dreams and the waking state—to unify our night perceptions with our day perceptions. Through the exercises of recognizing, multiplying, transforming, and unifying the dream with the clear light, we learn to be free of all grasping and clinging to unreal phenomena. Form is a dream and feeling is a dream; touch, sound, and taste are all dreams. The mental state is also dreamlike. Samsara and nirvana are dreams, and enlightenment is a great dream. Therefore, Guru Padmasambhava urges us to mingle our dream and waking realities. In truth, they are already mingled. There is ultimately no difference between them. As the Buddha instructed his disciple Subhuti in the Prajnaparamita teachings, "See all phenomena as dreams."

It's not just that the Buddha said this so we have to believe it. We can refer to our own experience. All these external activities are no different from dreams—no absolute distinction can be made between them, even when you consider it logically. For example, tonight we're in West Palm Beach. I'm talking and you're listening, but before this, where were you? Where are the parents you had when you were young? Where is your old school? What kinds of friends did you have? What did you talk about? What did you do? All of these are just memories now. We can't bring any of that right here except by remembering it. Last night's dream is just like those memories because we cannot produce it here in a tangible way. Memories are conventionally held to be real because they correspond with our past experiences in the waking state, while dreams are usually considered to be unreal. Investigate this closely—we don't think you'll find any difference between dreams and memories except in your imagination.

Consider how our physiology changes. As a newborn baby, we're not very heavy. Maybe we weigh six or seven pounds and are about a foot long. Yet we'll never be that small again. It is as if that happened in a dream. As for ourselves, we were born in Tibet and grew up there. We remember many events vividly, but they are all just memories. Tibet has completely changed since then. If we go back, we won't see anything that's the same. When we were a little older, we crossed the Himalayas and suffered various hardships until we finally arrived in India, where we lived for many years. Now all that has passed and another chapter of the dream is complete. Presently, we're in the United States working on a new chapter. You could say that in this life we've already been born three times! This is just a personal example, but basically this is how things are.

When we carefully observe phenomena, they are all dreamlike, but we don't often look that closely. We gloss over the surface and cling to our dualistic tendencies, reinforcing old habit patterns. In truth, even this moment is changing, moving, fleeting. There's nothing solid or permanent about any of this. What is past can never come back to the present. Everything is moving and nothing stays the same, just like in our dreams. For that reason, the Buddha compared the impermanent nature of all phenomena to a mirage, a magician's illusion, a bubble in a stream, and a flash of lightning.

This impermanence does not merely apply to things that happened long ago, but even to this morning's activities, which exist only in our memories. It's all gone now. That was just another dream sequence that we went through to get to this dream. This is the reality of the big dream.

As Vajrayana practitioners, we must redirect our minds. Continuous joyful effort is required to perform more positive activities, to gain more understanding, and to develop wisdom, loving-kindness, and compassion. The more we involve ourselves in this effort, the easier it is to transcend negative feelings and reactive emotions. Those who apply themselves in this way develop an uninterrupted insight into the body of enlightenment, the speech of enlightenment, and the wisdom mind of enlightenment. They see these three aspects of the Buddha all the time and have a deep understanding of their interplay. This same insight can also continue at night, in the dream state. When this happens, it means you have established your mind in the sphere of wisdom, beautified by love and compassion twenty-four hours a day.

Empowered with an understanding of the dream bardo, we can accomplish profound results and benefit all the dreamlike beings in samsara because we know we aren't truly limited by conventional structures and boundaries. If we generate tremendous vitality, courage, and commitment, liberating knowledge will manifest both in and out of dreams, transforming and benefiting everyone.

Since all phenomena are illusory, we are able to actualize the ultimate result. If things were really concrete and solid, we could never grow or develop. But because everything is dreamlike, it is possible for us to discover and reveal all the beautiful qualities of enlightenment and radiate blessings like sunlight to all beings. With this understanding, we can use dreaming to benefit others. On the other hand, if we do not know very much about the dreamlike nature of existence and try to find our original true nature out of ego-clinging, it will be an exercise in futility.

Third Bardo of Meditation

There are many types of meditation. All help the mind become more gentle, peaceful, and single-pointed so it is not disturbed by thoughts. As in dream yoga, every form of meditation must be based on our bodhichitta motivation and an awareness of our original purity. These two are always essential. Bodhichitta is the foundation, and awareness of our original purity is the inner structure of every practice.

When the meditation bardo is dawning upon me,
Abandoning all kinds of wandering and deluded
thoughts,
Remain in the state of nondistraction without clinging,
free from all limits.

Watch out for distractions, such as wandering or discursive thoughts. These are a great hindrance to meditation. Keeping your spine straight, maintain a comfortable posture, and let meditation deepen into a calm and clear state. Stay one-pointed, do not be distracted by conceptions, and continue maintaining your mind this way, whatever you're meditating on. That's basically it. As Guru Padmasambhava said, "No distractions, no grasping, and free of all aspects." These three qualities are essential to every form of meditation.

Right motivation and joyful effort are also indispensable. During meditation you will be faced with obstacles, clinging, compulsive thoughts and feelings, and other hindrances. To stay on target, meditate without distraction in the limitless expanse that transcends any territorial focus, the all-pervasive nature. Relaxing into this awareness is meditation.

Gain mastery of both generation and completion stages.

The division of meditation into creation (or generation) stage and completion stage practices is unique to Vajrayana Buddhism. These are the means for becoming firm and strong in our meditation.

Creation stage, or visualization practice, helps us to understand the purity of all phenomena, including ourselves, so that everything is perceived as the buddha mandala. This mandala is not a solidly existent thing. It's like a reflection, a mirage, a dream, or a rainbow. It is a wisdom display of clear light, the luminosity aspect of the true nature. Even in shorter Zhitro practices, all phenomena appear as the mandala of the peaceful and wrathful deities, and these deities dissolve into rainbow light; all speech and sounds are mantra, and all momentary thoughts are magical emanations of the open, spacelike nature of the sky. This understanding characterizes the creation stage meditation. This means that you are relatively free of clinging, holding, and grasping onto self and phenomena, and that you are skilled at merging with the true nature beyond all bias and limitations, where no dualities exist. Relaxing into this state of innate purity is the completion (or perfection) stage practice.

Awareness of purity can be developed by recognizing the preciousness of this human birth, the lineage teachings, and all sentient life. Indeed, every situation is very special. So see this, learn to appreciate and enjoy your experiences, and explore and celebrate the beauty in the world and in yourself. Discover the mandala and realize that the pureland is not far away. It's right here. According to the Zhitro teachings, the peaceful and wrathful deities do not exist externally—one's own body is the palace of the deities, and the entire universe is originally

The peaceful and wrathful deities
Vajrakilaya and Medicine Buddha Temple, Padma Samye Ling

in an enlightened state. Awaken to the preciousness and purity of each moment as it arises and devote yourself to maintaining this great realization. Guru Padmasambhava said:

In this moment of one-pointed meditation, abandon all activity . . .

Lay everything aside for the moment, even if it is for a good purpose.

And don't be influenced by deluded emotions.

Beware of indulging negative emotions. Guru Padmasambhava emphasizes this again because it is so crucial for the practice of meditation. For example, in the Vajrayana we meditate while visualizing Guru Padmasambhava and reciting his mantra, until finally Guru Padmasambhava dissolves into the primordial expanse as the wisdom lights at his crown, throat, and heart mingle completely with our own body, speech, and mind in a state of pure awareness. To abide in this purity is the completion stage meditation. This is the main part of the practice.

After that, dedicate the merit.* Whenever you feel you've done something good, do not hesitate to share the benefits with all sentient beings, without excluding anyone. Reaffirm your motivation of love and compassion, and finish the session by blessing all beings through the dedication prayers. Happily share this goodness with the entire world.

How will dedicating merit help us become enlightened? Sharing our good karma with all sentient beings opens our hearts and minds and expands our awareness of love and compassion. Directing the blessing to all beings without exception makes our prayers limitless. When no dualistic thoughts block our dedication, we approach the infinite nature of mind.

If we don't share in this way, if we don't feel love and compassion for all sentient beings, we're creating false divisions and will not grow

---

*A dedication prayer from the lineage is included in the appendix, or you may dedicate in your own words.

in our capacity to serve others. Eventually, these self-imposed bound-aries reduce us to a state of stubborn ego-clinging, which is where we were before we began to practice. Ego-clinging obscures our capacity for wisdom and denies us opportunities for meaningful involvement with others. Everything contracts into a static and fixed condition so that at times we cannot even help or protect ourselves, let alone others.

So always begin in the spirit of love, compassion, and bodhichitta. Meditate on the Buddha, recite the mantra, and finally dissolve the visualization while abiding in the true nature. At the end of each ses-sion keep your heart and mind open by dedicating the merit from the practice to all sentient beings. This is an extremely simple explanation of formal Vajrayana practice.

Since meditation is so important for us as Dharma practitioners, we'd like to discuss the essential points of meditation practice in more detail.*

Whenever we do any kind of Dharma practice, including medita-tion, the recitation of mantras, and sadhana practice, we should always begin with a great sense of joy and appreciation, along with awareness of the preciousness of time. This is very important. Presently we're enjoying very beautiful circumstances and situations and, for the most part, everything is quite good. Of course we also experience difficul-ties and rough situations. But it's important not to focus too much on these troubles and hardships. Instead, we should ignite more positive thoughts and attitudes by recognizing our many opportunities as well as the preciousness of our time here with joy and appreciation.

Our time in this world is not going to last forever; it will eventually run out. So there must be a sense of appreciation and urgency in our practice. Right now we have the wonderful opportunity to practice. We have time to practice. To some degree, appreciating this good fortune is part of renunciation. It touches very close to the truth of how we exist in the phenomenal world, the situations and circumstances in which we

*The following discussion of the essential points of meditation practice is adapted from an article in the 2007 spring/summer issue of the *Pema Mandala* magazine by the Ven-erable Khenpo Rinpoches entitled "Igniting the Beautiful Nature of the Teachings in Your Heart and Mind," which was edited by Andrew Cook and Lama Pema Dragpa.

find ourselves. Therefore, all of us should maintain joyous thoughts of appreciation very strongly in our hearts and minds. This is one of the best ways to sharpen our practice.

The second attitude that will strengthen our practice is bodhichitta. Bodhichitta is the sense of concern, caring, and consideration for all living beings, and it embodies the thoughts of love, compassion, and wisdom. Therefore it's essential to bring forth the dense power of bodhichitta in both our hearts and minds. In his teachings the Buddha often said, "Without compassion, the root of Dharma is rotten." Without compassion, the essence of the teachings is lost. In other words, bodhichitta is the very essence of the Dharma; compassion is the essence of our practice. Along with love, kindness, and compassion, the teachings often speak of the Four Boundless Qualities or Four Immeasurables, which are sympathetic joy and equanimity, and in addition to this, love and compassion. Bodhichitta is truly one of the most important aspects of our practice. Practicing in this way will definitely sharpen all our Dharma activities.

The third necessary attitude to develop our meditation practice includes devotion and faith. This is also known as taking refuge, which is the foundation of all schools of Buddhism. Our practice will not activate without these two closely linked qualities. Devotion refers to both trust and confidence, along with a feeling of comfort and closeness toward the Three Jewels, the Three Roots, and one's innate nature. Devotion and faith will make us feel happy and joyful toward practice. We have all received authentic practices, so we have everything we need. We can be confident that nothing is missing from the teachings we've been given, and there is no shortage of practices we can do!

Although we already have everything we need to progress along the path, our practice is lacking. Why? Because we're not using what we already have. We're not activating our renunciation of negative habits and cultivating bodhichitta, devotion, and faith. Therefore, we must continue to develop a close connection with the Three Jewels—Buddha, Dharma, and Sangha—as well as with Guru Padmasambhava and the lineage. This connection takes the form of a strong feeling of devotion, joy, closeness, and warmth. Trust and confidence are also very important. For all these reasons, devotion—which actually includes trust and confidence—will really help strengthen our practice of meditation as well as enhance all our activities, quickly bringing results. We could say that devotion is almost like adding MiracleGro to our practice! Truly, it is essential for our growth.

The next important attitude that will strengthen our practice involves mindfulness, alertness, and attentiveness or thoughtfulness. These qualities are all extremely important. One of the aims of Dharma practice, and Buddhism in general, is to improve ourselves. This means we need to improve and enhance our love, compassion, and wisdom. At the same time we're trying to reduce the strength and degree of our ego-clinging and negative emotions. The only way to do this is to look at ourselves. We are not the monitors of other people. As Buddhist practitioners, instead of always watching others and judging what they do, we have to watch our own minds and actions. This is known as mindfulness and alertness.

Simultaneously, we must develop patience. We shouldn't immediately place blame on others thinking that we are completely perfect. Putting others down and pointing out their shortcomings is a sign of weakness in a practitioner. Rather than clinging to this narrow view, we should activate our patience, alertness, and mindfulness. This will help us settle down so that we can really grow and develop. This is the next important technique that will strengthen our practice—treating both ourselves and others with patience.

To increase our patience it's necessary to examine our own errors and faults with the intention of removing and purifying them. We should think, *I'm not the perfect one here. I'm not perfect.* With this motivation we're trying to develop our good qualities and inner perfection so that we will eventually become good examples to others and be able to benefit them. By generating these qualities ourselves, we will become good practitioners. Patience and mindfulness are also excellent ways to increase our awareness in post-meditation and expand our bodhichitta.

Next, joyful effort is one of the most important qualities we can cultivate in order to sharpen our meditation practice. It's truly so important. Joyful effort isn't something to generate only once in a while, or every now and then. We cannot limit our practice to those times when we're feeling good, when things are going our way. Neither should we practice only when we experience difficulties and are going through rough times. It's crucial that we continue to practice until we fulfill the goal of complete enlightenment by fully developing our love, compassion, and wisdom.

Achieving the goal of supreme enlightenment for the benefit of all living beings is only possible by removing each and every one of our negative emotions, which serve only to harm ourselves and others. Therefore, we must continue to practice until we are free from all afflictive emotions and are no longer bothered by adverse circumstances. For example, we must practice until we don't become the slightest bit upset or irritated when somebody criticizes us. Similarly, we should practice until we have developed perfect equanimity, no longer clinging to either pleasure or pain, seeing them both as equal. Maybe we can slow down a bit once we reach this state. Until that time we should always practice diligently, with joyful effort and appreciation.

The teachings often warn us that we shouldn't just be practitioners when we're feeling good about ourselves and enjoying pleasant circumstances, boasting, "Oh, I am a good practitioner!" If we fall into this way of thinking, we'll lose our identity as practitioners the moment we undergo difficulties that interrupt our usual good times. We're not going to be bodhisattvas when we are having fun and then totally stop being bodhisattvas when we're experiencing difficulties. It doesn't work that way. A true bodhisattva is always consistent, whether he or she meets with pleasant or unpleasant circumstances.

Since this point is so important, we are going to explain it again: we have to continually apply joyful effort, courage and commitment, and perseverance and joy. In this way our practice will not fluctuate to extremes based on changing circumstances. Lacking joyful effort, we will be good practitioners only when our tummies are full, the sun is shining beautifully, and everything is quite okay. In other words, we will be good practitioners only as long as circumstances are moving along nicely, according to our wishes. Otherwise, the moment a small disturbance arises we completely lose our temper, becoming even worse than ordinary beings! This is not what it means to be a practitioner. The teachings definitely say this and it is really true. Perhaps we're having a good time on the beach and everything is nice—then we are really good practitioners. But when we're stuck in a traffic jam, it's really hot, and the air conditioner isn't working, we lose our practice. We must strive to be good practitioners in the traffic jam and on the beach.

This is why the teachings emphasize the importance of taming the mind. The true signs of accomplishment are when the mind continually remains gentle, peaceful, and content. In Tibet it's often said that it's wonderful if you can press a handprint or footprint in rock, but even more wonderful if you are always patient, loving, gentle, and peaceful. This is the greatest sign of achievement, the sign of a true practitioner. If you begin to experience these qualities more and more, it's a sure sign that your practice is working. So, patience, courage, and commitment are very helpful ways to strengthen our practice.

Next, we can enhance our practice by continuing to reduce the power of our attachments, which means letting go of our grasping and clinging. Visualization and dissolution stages of sadhana practice and meditation techniques such as shamatha and vipashyana are all designed to lessen our grasping and clinging so that we come to perceive all existing phenomena as dreamlike. These dream experiences themselves are also empty. So it is always important to apply these practices in order to lessen our grasping and clinging at the level of both subject and object.

Along with these techniques, acknowledging both our virtuous and nonvirtuous deeds is always very beneficial to our practice. We should feel happy and joyful whenever we're able to perform even a small meritorious activity. Likewise, we must acknowledge and purify even the smallest negative activity. Small causes can bring about very powerful results. The teachings of the Buddha advise us to immediately acknowledge and confess our negative actions as soon as we become aware of them. Think, *Oh, I did something bad. What I did was negative.* Acknowledging nonvirtuous activities as nonvirtuous is itself considered to be virtuous and good and will lead to wisdom. It implies that we are going to stop per-

forming negative actions next time. As we said, even this acknowledge-
ment itself is meritorious and should be dedicated.

In ancient times there was a householder named Chemdhag Palche.
The Buddha explained that thousands and thousands of lifetimes before
his birth as Chemdhag Palche, the man took rebirth as a pig. One day
the mud-covered pig was chased by a wild dog. During the chase the
pig brushed up against a stupa, filling up some of its cracks with mud.
The Awakened One taught that even this small, unintentional act
was virtuous, helping the pig accumulate merit. Therefore, it's good to
acknowledge and purify all negative activities while also acknowledging, rejoicing in, and dedicating all positive activities. We should use
our negativities as opportunities to purify our afflictive habit patterns,
and our virtuous activities to inspire ourselves. These are additional
methods for developing our practice.

As we mentioned earlier, the Buddha often taught that we should
dedicate the merit of each one of our positive actions to all living beings,
without partiality. This means we should dedicate even our tiniest virtuous and beneficial activities to the larger vision of enlightenment for
all sentient beings. At the present time our bodhichitta is very limited
when it comes to actualizing this love, compassion, and wisdom in a
tangible way in the service of living beings. However, our aspirational
bodhichitta is completely unimpeded. Therefore, we should dedicate
every one of our meritorious actions for the benefit of all living beings,
without discrimination, with the wish that our dedication immediately
frees them from all suffering and difficulties. By doing so, we make our
small actions part of the big picture, which is enlightenment for all parent beings as vast as space. While dedicating, we should not feel like
we're joking or that our dedication is ineffective. Sincerely wish from
the bottom of your heart that your dedication benefits everyone. Each
practice that we've discussed so far is virtuous, so dedicating all of these
beneficial actions for the benefit of others will secure our meritorious
activities and help increase our realization.

In terms of the Vajrayana creation and completion stage practices
(see glossary for a more detailed discussion of these practices), we
might wonder how we can connect more with the three vajra states

during creation stage practice. How do we see all forms as the body of the deity, hear all sounds as the recitation of the deity's mantra, and experience all conceptions as the play of the deity's wisdom mind?

It's true that we can experience doubt and hesitation during creation stage practice. Doubt can easily and naturally arise since this is the normal, mundane way we think. At these times, however, we should investigate the one who is visualizing the deity, such as Vajrasattva or Vajrakilaya.* This person is none other than mind itself. And we should ask ourselves, *Where is this mind?* Upon looking, we cannot pinpoint any location, since mind is empty. Therefore, all arising concepts such as *I am not really the deity* come from this empty mind.

Thoughts can come in many different forms, since the arising energy of mind is not regulated by anything. But during practice we're not going to follow the movement of any concepts, including doubts and hesitation. These are mere appearances of the emptiness of mind. Instead, we are going to bring forth confidence, thinking, *I am Vajrakilaya. Emptiness mind is the nature of Vajrakilaya.* From emptiness mind we arise as the deity, and we therefore perceive all phenomena as inseparable from the deity. In this way we usher forth our vajra pride, or natural confidence, and actually abide in the wisdom state. This is known as "connecting with the nature of mind."

We are allowing emptiness mind—our own awareness—to arise in the form of the meditational deity Vajrakilaya, which is also empty. Therefore, the entire universe of form and everything that we perceive is none other than the display of our own mind. Our mind is inseparable from Vajrakilaya, so we see everything from Vajrakilaya's perspective, unobscured by duality mind and unregulated by grasping and clinging. By practicing in this way we're going to immediately stop our habitual thought patterns of grasping and clinging, allowing the emptiness of mind to arise as the new, fresh perspective of Vajrakilaya.

Because there is no division between Vajrakilaya and our own mind, everything we hear is the sound of Vajrakilaya, and our awareness itself

---

*Vajrasattva is a buddha whose peaceful activities help sentient beings purify ego clinging. Vajrakilaya is a wrathful expression of this same buddha who helps uproot very stubborn, destructive habits with unconditional love, compassion, and wisdom.

Vajrakilaya, a wrathful deity who perfectly embodies
enlightened activities and removes obstacles that destroy
the forces hostile to compassion

Vajrakilaya and Medicine Buddha Temple, Padma Samye Ling

is the mind of Vajrakilaya. As the teachings say, the purpose of this
visualization is to destroy and uproot the solidity of our habitual patterns. Free from doubt and hesitation, practice the creation stage with
confidence and with recognition of the nature of mind.

What should we do if we have doubts about being able to truly relax in the completion stage? In general, the completion stage refers to going beyond all grasping and objects of thought. The essence of the completion state is Dzogchen meditation. To use the example we just gave, we should investigate where the visualization is coming from. Once again, these visualizations arise from emptiness mind. Yet when we investigate the location of mind itself—where it arises, where it abides, and where it ceases—we don't find anything, since there is no substantially existing mind. This "not finding" is Dzogchen. When we don't find mind, the not-finding itself is actually the state of Dzogchen. Simply relax and rest in this state without any second-guessing, free from doubts and hesitation.

We should also examine external objects. Following the logic of Madhyamaka,* we can analyze the nature of the objects of our perception. For example, "Where is this table?" When we break down the table in an attempt to find its essence, we eventually reach the atomic level. However, even the atoms themselves do not exist in a substantial or solid way. Actually, the entire universe is in this state: there is nothing substantially or solidly existing, no intrinsic core within any phenomena. Everything we normally perceive is a combination of causes, conditions, and hallucinations that combine to form our present perceptions. When we examine in this way we discover the empty nature of phenomena.

According to the teachings of the Vajrayana, during the completion stage everything dissolves into the deity, who then dissolves into the heart syllable of the deity. The heart syllable itself finally dissolves into the state of one's true nature. This means that every focal point we were previously holding in our awareness, including all the aspects of the visualization, dissolve back into the ultimate state of our true

---

*Madhyamaka, the "Middle Way," is one of many great Buddhist traditions (such as Madhyamaka, Mahamudra, and Dzogchen) that plumb the nature of reality. Madhyamaka is the philosophical stance embraced by Sutra and Tantra Mahayana Buddhists, which is founded on the doctrine of emptiness. Its essential purpose is to point toward a way of knowing that goes beyond the grasping of dualistic consciousness by introducing the absolute truth that is entirely beyond the limitations of conceptualization.

Garab Dorje
Padma Samye Ling gonpa murals

nature. There is nothing to focus on, and even our focus itself completely dissolves. Relax in the fresh, original, unfabricated state of the nature of mind. This is Dzogchen, the ultimate state of the completion stage. Resting in this state, there is no need for doubt, because mind has released all thought fabrications. We have reached the zero point, where even zero has disappeared. Just relax in this state. This is the completion stage of Dzogchen.

If you're an advanced practitioner, the moment you recognize the true nature of the mind—the primordial condition—you're totally enlightened. This ability is the mark of a yogi or yogini of the highest caliber. For example, upon recognizing the true nature of the mind, the famous Dzogchen master Garab Dorje was immediately and fully awakened. In other cases there is a very short interval between recognition and full enlightenment. After an initial realization of the true nature, these practitioners quickly learn to perceive all phenomena as a display of primordial

Vimalamitra

Padma Samye Ling gonpa murals

wisdom. Guru Padmasambhava, the great master Vimalamitra, and the Dzogchen master Shri Singha are examples of this second type of adept. They realized that they themselves and everything else are manifestations of primordial wisdom: the union of emptiness and appearances.

Other great masters from India and Tibet had to meditate for a long time before coming to this understanding. Through years of meditation and practice they became enlightened. In Tibet, there was a great master called Chetsun Senge Wangchuk, who meditated for seven years and attained the rainbow body. Pang Mipham Gonpo meditated for a long time and eventually realized the rainbow body. Master Netan Dangma Lhungyal meditated for about six years before actualizing the transcendental rainbow body. All of these masters practiced meditation for years before attaining the rainbow body of transcendental wisdom.

Shri Singha

Padma Samye Ling
gonpa murals

**Chetsun Senge
Wangchuk**

Padma Samye Ling
gonpa murals

The bardo of meditation is actually a very big topic. All of the bardos are encompassed by the meditation bardo because it is only through meditation that we can come to recognize the true nature in all the other bardos. Once we awaken to our true nature, the confusion of the bardos comes to an end.

Fourth Bardo of Dying

Life is followed by the bardo of dying or the moment of death. Death is an inevitable part of this highway we travel. All compounded things dissolve. Birth is followed by life and then death; that is the natural sequence of existence for all beings. Things arise, abide for a moment, and then decay. Nothing and no one is exempt. This is true for us also. It's only a question of when it will happen. Someone may have a relatively longer or shorter amount of time left, but every creature who ever lived has died. Worldly power, beauty, and wealth will not prevent it. Although we tend to fear it, death is not evil, but a natural transformation that we've all been through many times. Death serves the renewal of life and is a necessary part of reality until we realize buddhahood.

Many great masters have written in their songs that we only die because we're ready to take another birth. This is part of an ongoing process, where one form of experience follows another, uninterruptedly. As number one passes, number two arises. Die bravely and peacefully, be happy with what you have achieved. Go joyously. This kind of inspired acceptance of death is necessary, even for ordinary people. Practice and meditation will help us learn to die with awareness, to recognize the true nature and merge with the visions that arise after death. These abilities are an invaluable result of a life of practice.

To die satisfied and peacefully is crucial to a good passage. Let go of any fears or regrets. Do not be sad or hold on to any sense of loss or separation. Meanwhile, in this current bardo of life, learn about this process and prepare yourself in order to make a smooth transition. By studying and contemplating the bardo of dying now we can preview the obstacle course and learn to act appropriately and courageously through every stage, without being distracted by the futility of hopes and fears.

THE ELEMENTS

We are born and live amidst the five elements: earth, water, fire, wind, and space. Space pervades all the other elements—it is everywhere. The Buddha taught that the formation of the world is based on space, followed by strong wind energy, fire, water, and earth. All internal and external phenomena—everything we perceive, the objects we use, our bodies, the places we stay, and the food we eat—are composed of these five elements. We are intimately involved with the elements, and if any of them are out of balance it can cause serious trouble.

The health of a flower garden and all the trees depend on this balance. We all have some idea of the complex interplay of elements that make up our external environment. This is the same system that makes up our bodies. The slightest imbalance can lead to sickness. When the elements no longer coordinate and finally disintegrate, we call it "death." In the Self-Arising Awareness Tantra, Guru Padmasambhava gave extensive Dzogchen teachings on the interrelations between the internal and external elements, describing how they function and dissolve.

In our body, our flesh, bones, and muscles are all part of the earth element. Blood, mucus, and other liquids are part of the water element. Vital warmth or bodily heat is due to the fire element. Breath, circulation, and all movements depend on the wind element. Consciousness, or mind, is considered part of the sky or space element. All the open, uncompounded spaces within the body are no different than the space that is occupied by the universe of forms, such as the sun and moon.

These five elements comprise the basic ground of this world. When we die, the five elements dissociate and our body disintegrates. The vitality that brought them together no longer has the energy to organize and maintain them in this form, so the elements are released back into the universe. When only consciousness is left, death has occurred.

CHAOS IN THE WINDS

The primary signs indicating the onset of death are caused by the dissolution of the elements. Most of the time these changes reflect the natural degeneration of the bodily systems under the influence of age and disease. The Dzogchen teachings of Guru Padmasambhava state that the wind element is the foundation of our physical system. Wind takes the principal role in establishing, maintaining, and building up the body. The winds give rise to all the chakras and channels. The first sign of impending death manifests as a growing disorder in the wind system. When the winds are disturbed, the other elements are immediately affected, and dissolution begins.

At the moment of conception, a subtle mind consciousness and wind unite to fuse the essence elements of the father and the mother into a zygote. The wind continues to organize the elements as the embryo begins to develop. The force of that wind creates all the major channels, distributes the elements, and develops the nervous and circulatory systems. Basically, we have five primary winds: (1) the life force wind is connected to the heart, keeping it strong to continue pumping blood; (2) the upward moving wind sustains the breath, helping us inhale oxygen and exhale gases we don't need; (3) the downward wind processes the materials we can't use and expels them; (4) the wind of fire helps digest food and sends it to whatever parts of the body need it; (5) the pervasive wind is like a reserve army that backs up the other wind systems and pervades the whole body. When we begin to die, the normal course of these winds is disrupted.

First, the pervasive wind becomes disordered and all movement becomes difficult. Your whole body may develop a numbness, and your hands and legs won't move easily. This in turn affects the life force wind. When this happens, the mind becomes clouded and frightened because it can't identify objects or see well. Imbalance spreads, disrupting the downward wind system. It becomes difficult to control your bowels. This affects the upward wind so that shortness of breath may develop. Finally, the equalizing heat of digestion is upset. With the disorder of the wind of fire, bodily warmth disperses and the feet and hands grow cold. Body temperature gradually drops, which also contributes to poor digestion.

Such experiences usually indicate the onset of death, and although conditions could change, most of the time these signs indicate that consciousness is preparing to depart from the body. As disorder increases in the wind system, it creates disturbances in the channels and chakras. The first effect of this relates to the navel chakra.

Body with chakras and channels

Line drawing by Khenchen Palden Sherab Rinpoche

EARTH DISSOLVES INTO WATER

The navel is the primary root of the body. When you are conceived and start to form in your mother's womb, the body develops through the movement of winds that emanate from the channel at the navel. During the process of dissolution, the changes begin where they originally started, in the movement of the winds associated with the navel chakra. As the navel chakra begins to disintegrate, the winds grow more out of balance until the earth element begins to quake.

Three signs will arise when the navel chakra begins to cease functioning: an outer sign; an inner sign; and a secret sign. The most external sign is that your body becomes extremely heavy. When all five wind systems are in disorder, this has an immediate effect on the navel chakra, causing your body to feel very heavy and stiff. This is a result of the earth element dissolving into the water element. It also indicates that the pancreas, which is associated with the earth element, is malfunctioning. The person dying may not be able to hold up their hand if you pick it up and let it go. They cannot walk without support. Their complexion becomes very pale, and you may see dark spots on their teeth.

The inner sign is that their mind becomes dull, lacking clarity or stability. Consciousness seems to be fading or sinking. In response to this, the person may try to take off their clothes, feeling that this will help them feel lighter or more awake. They may seem to be hot, but this is really in response to the changes happening within. They may ask to be lifted or supported with a higher pillow to counter the feeling of sinking. These are the inner signs of dissolution. Help them get comfortable and reassure them that everything is fine. If they're a practitioner, remind them of their practice, the Dharma, and their beliefs. No matter what school they belong to, create a peaceful environment full of love and compassion. Even if the person is not interested in the Dharma at all, serve him or her as they like—the best thing you can do is to help ease their mind. Don't think that the Dharma is so great that you have to force it on anyone. This is the time to work with the person's interests and passions. Be calm and peaceful and try to soothe and relax the dying person. Help them be courageous. This is crucial. Use kind words and speak with respect. Do whatever will help ease and comfort them.

The secret sign consists of a miragelike experience. It may seem to the person that everything, even the external environment, is flowing and moving. Things may appear closer or farther away than they actually are. Vision becomes undependable. Guru Padmasambhava compared this to seeing a scintillating mirage moving across the landscape in the springtime. These secret signs are all aspects of primordial luminosity. Though not continual, the person dying might experience a mirage of haze in the sky, and subtle, peripheral movements, as if fleas were jumping around. These visions won't stay very long and mark the first appearance of the luminosity of the true nature.

Technically, you could say there are two bardos here: the bardo of dying as well as a secret revelation of the fifth bardo of the luminosity of the true nature. At this time, they share such a thin border that we can hardly distinguish between them. In fact, the luminosity bardo is secretly happening even before the dissolution of the elements in the bardo of birth and life. The secret signs happen quickly and don't take as long as the external and internal signs do. Thus begins the dissolution of the elements. During this time it is very important for the person and those around him or her to create a quiet, peaceful environment with as few negative emotions as possible.

WATER EVAPORATES INTO FIRE

As the water element evaporates into the fire element, the heart chakra begins to disintegrate. There are outer, inner, and secret signs associated with this phase as well. The external sign is that the mouth and respiratory passages become very dry and the nostrils constrict. The tongue becomes dry and difficult to move. The brightness of the complexion is gone. The kidneys are beginning to not work properly. It's helpful to offer the person some water or a moistened cloth at this point.

The inner sign is strongly experienced by the person who is undergoing the dying process. The mind becomes unstable, and he or she may feel agitated, moody, frustrated, and a little frightened. Awareness can be quite sharp and precise at times, but in other moments there is no clarity and the mind is very dull. These states shift back and forth in an irregular way so that the dying person might become a little short-tempered or even angry.

The secret sign is a vision of smoky, blue-grey clouds repeatedly forming and dissolving. This will not last very long, but it may happen often. Again, these are signs of the primordial luminosity. The smoky visions occur when the kidneys, which are associated with the water element, cease to function. During this phase, continue to make the person who is dying feel loved and appreciated. Offer them support and encouragement. Create a harmonious environment. If the person is a practitioner, remind them of their particular wisdom deity. If the dying person is not a Buddhist, kindly support whatever source of refuge brings them comfort and peace, and help them maintain a continuous meditation. This is extremely important.

FIRE DISSIPATES INTO WIND

As the fire element is dispersed by the wind element, disorder moves from the heart chakra to the speech chakra. The outer sign of this transition is that the hands, feet, and breath become cold. Heat is radiating away from the body, gradually cooling toward the heart center, as the fire element dissolves into the wind element.

There may be hot and cold flashes, which finally settle into cold. Once in a while you will see a mist or vapors rising off the dying person. The immune system disintegrates, the liver stops functioning, and it becomes difficult to make distinctions between good and bad.

The inner sign associated with the disorder of the speech chakra is that the mind and vision become even more blurred and unstable. The dying person may recognize friends and family one minute, but not the next.

The secret sign associated with the luminosity of the true nature is an inner vision similar to the flashing of lightning bugs.

These stages of dissolution may not last a long time, but they generally proceed in this order. Become familiar with the sequence so that during the process of dissolution you're able to recognize all the signs and courageously go forward. It's also very important for everybody present to be free of anger and attachment, because these attitudes are big obstacles to the person who is dying.

WIND DIFFUSES INTO CONSCIOUSNESS

As the wind element dissolves into the space of consciousness, the secret chakra* becomes disordered. The body shakes, movement becomes unsteady, and then is completely out of control. The external signs associated with this transition are a lengthening of the breath, accompanied by a subtle rattle. Speech becomes unclear and mumbled. It becomes difficult to inhale and exhale. The lungs are collapsing. The eyes may roll upward.

The inner sign of this stage is that the mind is no longer quite as agitated but is still very unstable. The person may feel quite happy one moment and sad or a little angry the next. The emotions are continually changing. One may experience a rapid visionary display of the habit patterns and emotions characterizing the most recent lifetime. For example, if the dying person has been a good practitioner, she will have a sublime experience of love and compassion. A person with nonvirtuous habits will have quite another experience. If he has any good karma, he may feel remorse and ask for help getting over it at this stage. Vivid memories arise momentarily and disappear, before returning in new combinations. It's similar to the headline news in review. The nature of one's habit patterns is made quite clear during this period.

Advanced practitioners will now see the Buddha or Guru Padmasambhava, so they are not afraid and are even able to enjoy the process of dissolution and be happy. Simply reciting some mantras while beholding the lama, the mind is peaceful and relaxed. The equanimity this engenders can be seen outwardly as well. The specific details of this phase depend on the activities performed during one's lifetime.

---

*The secret chakra is located in the reproductive area and deals with the life force.

The secret sign of this stage is a vision of many glowing lights in different places. They are very small but they do not blink on and off like lightning bugs. This is the fourth vision of primordial luminosity. At this point, the lungs cease functioning. The lungs correspond to the wind element, which is dispersing into the space of consciousness. When the lungs cease to function, one exhales the last breath, and that's it. The person's heart center still maintains some heat, and that is where consciousness finally dissolves. This marks the last stage of the bardo of dying.

CONSCIOUSNESS DISSOLVES INTO CLEAR LIGHT

The four gross elements have all dissolved. Some teachings explain that after the wind element dissolves into consciousness, consciousness dissolves into the sky—the luminosity of the true nature—which is great openness. The movement of the breath has stopped. The five senses are inactive. There's no ego-consciousness, so one's eyes, ears, nose, tongue, and body consciousnesses are all interrupted. This is known as the completion stage. At this point, nothing is experienced outside of yourself—it's all completely within. You see that everything you perceive is mind and nothing else. Your perception completely dissolves into the clear light.

Although living people can still perceive the world, the person dying no longer registers external stimuli. For the moment, that is all over. External appearances dissolve, and although at the level of consciousness there are still a few more transitions to go through, all dualistic concepts and thinking are suspended. There's no longer any activity.

In the case of a practitioner who understands the visualization (creation) and completion stages, recognition of each inner and secret sign helps them perfectly abide in the process of enlightenment. Through practice, you can merge your mind with the visions of luminosity the moment they arise. This is a very powerful time and one of the best chances to realize our buddha nature. We don't even have to meditate to generate these things; the inner and secret signs will all arise naturally.

Practice prepares us to connect at any point. Clear recognition of even the first secret sign can lead directly to enlightenment.

These are Guru Padmasambhava's bodhichitta teachings on the nature of mind, revealing the details of what we'll have to face during and after death. It's kind of like an airline attendant showing us how to use the life jackets and escape ramps. But unlike most airline passengers, every one of us will definitely have to make this exit. That's why we're considering all of this in some detail. Guru Padmasambhava said that we should deal with the bardo of dying like a beautiful woman going to the market. She doesn't have any doubts or fears about her attractiveness. She's already very beautiful, but she still checks herself one last time before she leaves the house to ensure that her hair and makeup are perfect. Similarly, we should prepare for death by developing a strong practice, so that when the time comes, we too can make one last check and then move forward with great courage, dignity, and happiness.

What we've discussed here relates to the gradual process of the dissolution of the elements that we call "dying." Now we'll continue with what happens after death.

WHITE, RED, AND BLACK VISIONS

By this time the dying person has stopped communicating with the external world. She no longer sees forms, hears sounds, smells odors, tastes flavors, or feels anything. There is no awareness of any sense objects.

Although breathing has stopped, there is still a subtle wind or inner breath present, so consciousness is still associated with the body. Occasionally people have come back to life from this point because until the inner breath stops there's a slight chance one could revive. At this time the white and red elements begin to vibrate toward disintegration. The inner experience of this phase is associated with three visions: a white vision, a red vision, and a black vision.

The white and red elements, which we received from our parents in the form of sperm and egg, are known as the root elements of the body. The white essence, which we got from our father, pervades the body but

Upside-down
HAM syllable

mainly resides within the crown chakra. The red essence, received from our mother, is also found throughout the body but is concentrated in a place about four finger-widths below the navel chakra. As these two elements drift toward disorder, the white element is affected first.

In the form of an upside-down syllable HAM, the white element will start to descend down the central channel from the crown chakra to the heart center. HAM is a syllable with the power of inducing a sense of shock to the system. We make sounds like HA and HO when there is any energy surging through the crown because the white HAM that resides there is stimulated into motion. As the crown chakra begins trembling, the white element starts dripping down through the central channel toward the heart center. At this time the dying person will experience bright moonlight radiating through everything, flashing silvery-white. For a short time, everything goes white, like when lightning strikes. This is the fifth experience of the clear light of reality, which is known as *nangwa*, or the "vision of brightness."

A few seconds, or perhaps a minute, after the descent of the white element, the downward winds begin to shake and dislocate the red element from its residence four finger-widths below the navel chakra.

Red AH syllable

Calligraphy by Ven. Khenpo Tsewang Dongyal Rinpoche

In the form of a red AH syllable, the red element begins ascending toward the heart. As it starts rising, the dying person will experience a crimson vision the color of flames, or the deep red of the sky before dawn. In Tibetan this is called *chepa*, the eruption or vision of burning fire. This is the sixth appearance of the clear light of the true nature.

When the white element—contributed by the father—begins to drip from the crown down to the heart, all anger dissolves. When the red element comes up from below the navel and merges with the heart, attachment comes to an end. The thirty-three emotions associated with anger and the forty emotions related to attachment all cease.

Now comes the seventh vision, known in Tibetan as *topa*, or the completing vision. When the red and white elements merge at the heart, consciousness is trapped between them. Finally, the two elements dissolve. At this point your vision goes black, like the new moon. This darkness is the seventh vision of primordial luminosity. Simultaneously, the seven ignorant emotions completely stop, and all eighty gross emotions are inactivated. A few seconds after you have the black vision you enter a state that is similar to being unconscious. You don't have any more visions or experiences—it's as if you've fainted. This doesn't just happen to human beings; it even happens to animals when they die.

The mind goes completely blank for a short time as consciousness settles in the clear light. Most beings stay in this space for a few seconds or minutes, but not much longer.

Very soon afterward, an eighth experience, called "regaining vision," arises, which is called *nyertob* in Tibetan. This is simply consciousness waking up again. The eight subtle winds that are naturally part of the mind begin to stir, and rays of primordial wisdom radiate, waking you up. The moment you come to, you are in the absolute state of the true nature, beyond conception, free of all complexity and emotion and awake in the naked brilliance of pristine cognition. You experience it directly now, unobscured by subject-object dualism. Clear and bright beyond description, this is an unconditional experience of the absolute reality of the true nature.

Through meditation practice you may have had some experience of the true nature while alive. But due to the dissolution of the different elements, it is clearly revealed at this time, free of any physical, mental, or emotional barriers. If you practice regularly during life, your recognition in this moment will be free of error, hesitation, and doubt. You will fearlessly and effortlessly mingle your awareness with the true nature, like a child crawling up onto her mother's lap. If you're able to do that, you will attain enlightenment in the bardo of the moment of death.

In the Dzogchen tantras, there are very subtle teachings about this experience. In The Prayer to Actualize the Pure Land of the Three Kayas, the master Jigme Lingpa describes clear light awareness as the most pristine openness, transparent as an autumn sky free of dust, clouds, and wind. There is no longer any notion of a separate self or an external world. All is perfectly unified in natural, unqualified awareness. One is completely liberated by recognizing this nondual state, thereby merging the dharmadhatu (absolute wisdom) with the primordial ground. In the colophon to this beautiful prayer, Jigme Lingpa explains that he wrote it while meditating in the mountains near Samye Monastery. Early one morning he walked outside, and while gazing at Mount Hepori, he thought of how Guru Padmasambhava and his twenty-five disciples had done many practices there on behalf of the BuddhaDharma almost a thousand years before. Reflecting on this, he thought, *Now we only have the history of these events because almost everything from those days is gone. As for myself, someday I too will be a part of history or just a memory. Therefore I should try to realize all phenomena as a manifestation of the three kayas, so that I don't have to suffer this movement through time.* Then he composed this prayer spontaneously.

Dzogchen practitioners can be classified into high, middle, and low levels. These levels are sometimes translated as "advanced," "intermediate," and "beginner." The higher two levels of practitioners won't have to go through the bardos and so won't need to apply these techniques. These instructions are for ordinary beings who will have to go through all the bardo transitions and experiences. This also applies to lower practitioners who may have already received a lot of teachings but so far have been unable to actualize the real meaning. Practitioners usually have a wider horizon of spiritual opportunities, more vitality, and better vision in the bardos than nonpractitioners. But low-level practitioners and ordinary people are classified together here because even though they might handle them differently, both will have similar experiences.

The highest of the low-level practitioners can realize the dharmakaya the moment it arises on the basis of having meditated and practiced while alive. If they weren't able to fully realize the true nature while alive, they have at least become intimate with it through meditation, so that after death they can easily identify and enjoy the blissful luminosity of pristine cognition, free of obstacles, impurities, or impediments. Their awareness merges with that clear light realization in the dharmakaya.

Having practiced during life, the practitioner finally sees what he or she has been meditating on and fully merges with that understanding. This is enlightenment, or realization of the dharmakaya—the absolute condition described in the Prajnaparamita teachings as "inconceivable, inexpressible, unborn and unceasing, by nature like the sky, experienced by self-reflexive awareness' discerning pristine cognition."

We meditate in order to realize the essential meaning expressed in the Heart Sutra: "Emptiness is form and form is emptiness." Release all conceptions and abide in the sphere of pristine awareness. In the moment immediately after death, there is a direct seeing. It's not like you're meditating and happen to have a vision. This time you're seeing the nature of mind as it really is.

Most of the time, gross conceptions block our true vision so that meditation does not penetrate as deeply as we'd like it to. There's always a feeling of separation: the duality of a self and whatever it is we're meditating on. But in the bardo of the luminosity of the true nature there is no feeling of separation. We enjoy complete freedom from the eighty emotional conceptions. There are no hindrances; we see everything clearly and vividly through direct perception. As you deepen your practice during this lifetime you will be able to merge your mind with the original brightness of rigpa, free of the usual notion of a separate self.

For example, if during life you were able to meditate one-pointedly for five minutes, you might stay in awareness of the true nature for five minutes. If you could remain in meditation for one week, you can extend this phase for a week. If you can only stay undistracted for one minute, you might last a minute. These periods are referred to as "meditation days," indicating the average length of time that you're able to remain in meditation. If you have not cultivated any meditative equanimity during your life, you probably won't be able to remain in the clear light for more than a second or two before you begin the next phase.

In the Dzogchen teachings it's said that primordial wisdom arises fresh and naked, without any coverings or shields. By recognizing it at this time we make all further bardo experiences unnecessary. This is the best opportunity to gain enlightenment in the dharmakaya, but if we're somehow unable to recognize this opening, a further experience of primordial luminosity arises.

It becomes progressively harder from here. Pristine cognition is free of negative emotions. It begins open, fresh, peaceful, tranquil, and clear. But as you slowly come back into the world of duality, subtle complexities begin to arise. The eighty emotions that had temporarily disappeared start to return.

Following these stages of dissolution, an ordinary person with no meditative experience or spiritual knowledge will enter a state of overall dullness for a short time, after having been frightened, irritated, agitated, and so on. Dharma practitioners, even though they may not be totally realized, can track every step. Their recognition of these signs allows them to merge the process of dissolution with the path. If they are fully aware of everything and can maintain that awareness, they can be in a state of constant meditation. In particular, toward the end of the process of dissolution, the mind becomes a bit more settled. At first this stability is irregular, but it gradually becomes continuous. By recognizing the signs, awareness can be easily maintained.

When great practitioners die, they become enlightened. But even ordinary people who are just beginning to understand these processes can make good progress toward realization. If there is any wisdom in relation to the stages of dissolution, the mind will be more settled and calm. This peace allows one to handle the situation quite well.

The dissolution process could pass in one day, although subjectively it is experienced as being much longer. To the dying person, it can seem like months or weeks, when really it may only last for an hour. What we have explained here applies to a gradual process of dissolution. An accidental or sudden death doesn't always allow enough time for the outer, inner, and secret signs to manifest. Even in the case of a natural death, the bardo teachings say that you can experience the secret signs very quickly, particularly the final signs of the white, red, and black experiences caused by the disorder of the white and red elements.

THE WAY OF GREAT MEDITATORS

High-level practitioners don't have to go through any of the bardo transitions. When they are dying they already have a good understanding of the true nature and are aware that everything is part of the mind. Although their body is dying, they are actually merging with the dharmakaya. For such yogis and yoginis, death is a process of releasing the old, habitual bindings associated with their body. They fully realize primordial wisdom, and their awareness continues to manifest on that basis. This is not the ordinary way of dying; they have a private exit. They don't go through all the transitions that nonpractitioners have to go through.

It's traditional to use the example of the space contained by a vase. When the vase is broken, the inner space and the outer space intermingle without boundaries. Nothing happens except a natural merging of space into space. So it is with those who understand the true nature—the moment they leave the body, they merge with the heart of Buddha Samantabhadra in great Dzogchen realization, free from the stains of birth and death. This is great enlightenment. For these sublime beings, death is not a time of sadness and sorrow, but of supreme happiness.

At death, the greatest Dzogchen practitioners show what are known as the "four highest signs of realization," indicating that they have reached enlightenment:

- The moment when the most enlightened yogis and yoginis abandon their bodies they dissolve in transcendental wisdom and acquire the rainbow body. Their awareness merges with the dharmakaya, and their bodily elements are transformed into transcendental wisdom energy, like the substance of a rainbow. This is also known as the "transcendental wisdom body."

- Others leave their body in a blaze of light or a heap of flames. Sometimes it is white light, sometimes blue or green. Occasionally they display a multicolored light of white, yellow, red, blue, and green. This light stays for a short time and then disappears. People see the fire, but when it is through burning there is no trace of a body, bones, or ash. It all just dissolves. These are definite signs of enlightenment. Such practitioners have awakened to their true nature and gain full realization the moment they leave their body. They merge with the luminosity of the clear light in the sambhogakaya.

- The third class of accomplished practitioners attain buddhahood in the nirmanakaya. As soon as they depart their bodies, they merge with the luminosity of the true nature. Externally, you might see light, fire, water, or other elements dissolve into the nirmanakaya. For example, when the Dzogchen master Garab Dorje died, he was immediately transformed into light. His foremost student,

Manjushrimitra, yearned longingly for him, and in that moment he saw his master's right hand stretch out from a sphere of light in the sky and drop a small cask containing the text of the oral instruction known as "The Three Words that Strike the Crucial Point." This was Garab Dorje's final Dzogchen testament, which he gave to Manjushrimitra before he disappeared, and it exemplifies the third extraordinary way of dying.

- The fourth type of death is known as the way of dakini transformation. As soon as awareness departs from the body, it disappears, and only the nails and hair remain. Everything else dissolves. There are also great masters whose body size decreases after death. After three days or a week, the body begins to shrink until it totally disappears except for the nails and hair.

All of these processes are associated with the actualization of the rainbow body. This is the highest way to leave the body. Many Dzogchen masters in India and Tibet become enlightened by meditating on the class of instructions of Dzogchen called *Longde*, or "Space Division,"* and thereby achieve the rainbow body. During the days of Guru Padmasambhava, the eighty-four mahasiddhas all attained rainbow bodies at the time of their deaths. Seven generations of practitioners in the lineage of Vairochana also enjoyed this attainment, as well as Shri Singha and Manjushrimitra. We have even heard more recent news from India about people attaining similar realization. In the Buddha's teachings, the attainment of the rainbow body is equivalent to enlightenment or buddhahood. This is the way of death for great meditators in the Dzogchen tradition, where the rainbow body is a well-known phenomena. It's a sign that after realizing buddhahood, you don't just disappear into space; you begin to act spontaneously for the good of all sentient beings.

Those who do not attain the rainbow body but are nevertheless advanced practitioners don't hesitate when it's time to die. They are beyond hope and fear and don't make any big deal about dying. They

---

*Longde is that part of the Dzogchen teachings that emphasizes spaciousness or emptiness.

simply die and attain enlightenment. These courageous beings let go like babies. They have no regrets, and they're not worried or sad. Without any plans or expectations, they don't have any thought about what they like or don't like. Having seen through the distinctions between life and death, they are not attached to staying here and are unafraid to die. They just go naturally wherever they happen to be, whether up in the mountains, near glaciers, or down in green valleys—they die like lions, without any fear. Although they appear to be experiencing death, they're actually leaping from samsara to enlightenment. This is why

Manjushrimitra, one of the early masters
of the Dzogchen lineage
Padma Samye Ling gonpa murals

Guru Padmasambhava and other masters taught that such practitioners are not really dying; they are perfectly released into full awakening. This manner of death applies to all those of the highest capacity. Those who have developed spiritual awareness and mindful equanimity do not experience any bardo after death.

Most practitioners of Mahamudra and Dzogchen leave the body through the central channel. This indicates a degree of control over the mind, allowing them to choose the direction and destination of their next rebirth. Those who can merge with clear light awareness might remain in the meditative posture. Some drop their heads forward, but most don't, and they stay in meditation anywhere from three days to a week. This is a sign that they have merged with the primordial luminosity.

In Tibet it's quite common for practitioners to pass away in meditation posture. They sit exactly as they sat in meditation during their lifetime so that they resonate with their practice. They merge their awareness completely with the true nature, while externally remaining in meditation. Their complexion remains very bright and clear, and many times their skin stays supple. It can almost even seem like they're still breathing.

When the consciousness leaves through the top of the central channel, the head drops and often you see a little blood drain from the left nostril, or clear liquid might come from the right nostril. You'll also find a clear or whitish liquid mixed with some blood coming out of the lower part of the urinary tract. These are signs that the consciousness has left the body via the wisdom wind. It's very important to not disturb the deceased person at this time. Be quiet and don't touch them so they're not distracted.

In the 1960s, when we first arrived in Darjeeling, India, there was a lama who died in the hospital. He stayed in the meditation posture after death. Some Indians thought he was still alive and had just fainted, so they tried to resuscitate him. Others realized that he had died and was in meditation and advised that he be left alone. Before long his head dropped and it was clear that he had died. When we asked who he was, we learned that he was not a master, but an ordinary Nyingma-Kagyu practitioner who apparently had good realization.

To die with clarity and full awareness, free of any external complications, is one of the favorite themes expressed in the teaching songs of masters. Once Milarepa said he would be very happy to die alone in a cave, with nobody there to ask, "How are you feeling?" He boldly sings, "Let me die here with no one to lament my passing or to see my corpse afterwards." In our own time it was the fifteenth day of the eleventh month of the Fire Tiger year, January 14, 1987, when His Holiness Dudjom Rinpoche said to his wife and those close to him, "Now I have completed everything." Usually he would do all his regular practices and meditate and pray for people who requested his prayers in many directions, but on this day he said, "I have completed everything, every prayer that has been asked of me. Now I'm going to leave. Please be careful in the future to pay attention. Karma can be very subtle and tricky. We might think something is no big deal, but it may turn out to have serious consequences, so pay good attention to the karmic process. This is what every practitioner needs to pay attention to—even those with the highest realization. I've done my part." Upon hearing this, many of those present didn't believe him. They thought he was making some casual statement. But soon afterward he got sick and passed away. This is how the great ones move on.

MANDALA OFFERINGS AT THE TIME OF DEATH AND DYING

In Tibet, many practitioners have very few possessions. Others have more things, such as money, property, and loved ones, to which they might cling and feel attached. Do not dwell on attachments or succumb to ego-clinging, anger, or fear. Particularly at the time of death, try to avoid these attitudes and generate more courage and joy by mentally making mandala offerings to Buddha Shakyamuni, Guru Padmasambhava, and especially to Buddha Amitabha.

Here in the West, it's customary to make out a will. If done in the spirit of bodhichitta, this exercise can help you prepare to give up attachments. When you see that your time has come, consider all the valuables that you're leaving behind, collect them in your mind, and make a beautiful mandala offering to Buddha Amitabha. Give away everything without exception in your last moments. The merit of your generosity will accompany you.

If you know the mandala prayer, do it as you offer up everything. Say, "I offer my body, speech, and wealth, my belongings and everything else to Buddha Amitabha. Please accept these offerings and lead me to enlightenment on the bodhisattva path, so that I can benefit all sentient beings. May I fully understand this process and enter the dharmakaya. Please support and help me through these changes." Meditate and cherish these thoughts, and offer everything to Amitabha. Once you do this, you should no longer feel regret or attachments to any belongings or people, because once you give them to the Buddha, there is no need to cling to them. You don't have to think about them any more since you already gave them up! It is similar in Tibet with torma offerings used in ceremonies. Once you offer the tormas, which are small sculptures made of flour and butter, you don't care what happens to them or who takes them. It's no longer your concern.

Dying peacefully and happily, in a detached state of mind, means without any sense of having left anything unfinished. Feel that everything has been completed. By sincerely making this offering, you will move beyond fear and can joyfully begin the process of death.

If you don't know how to visualize the mandala offering, concentrate on Buddha Amitabha or Guru Padmasambhava. Feel their presence and look forward to this great transition. In the root text, Guru Padmasambhava wrote:

> *When the bardo of the moment of death is dawning upon me,*
> *Abandoning attachment and clinging to everything,*
> *Remain in the sphere of the clear instructions.*

This is the time to remember your teacher's pith (essential) instructions, the heart essence of the practice. Refresh your memory and remind yourself of the key points.

There are two main stages of application in the Vajrayana: the creation stage and the completion stage. The creation stage practices involve seeing every form in the universe as the body of the buddhas, hearing all sounds as the speech of the buddhas, and knowing every level of awareness—and even space itself—as the mind of the buddhas. This is to help you stabilize your understanding that you are already enlightened—it's simply a matter of continuously abiding in that awareness and clearly recognizing all things in the sphere of pristine cognition.

The completion stage practice is referred to as "beyond coming and going." If somehow you aren't able to maintain this understanding, then

Mandala offering
Main shrine in Padma Samye Ling gonpa

just meditate and visualize buddhas and bodhisattvas in the space in front of you. Or visualize yourself as a deity and relax in the inconceivable expanse of the true nature and remain there, confident in liberation, full of love and compassion, calm and peaceful. This is another way to practice the completion stage.

PHOWA, TRANSFERENCE OF CONSCIOUSNESS

The moment of death is the time to implement phowa practice for the transference of consciousness. There is nothing arbitrary about when to do phowa. If your practice is on a high level and you already see everything in the three vajra states of pure body, pure speech, and pure mind, it will not be necessary to perform phowa—you've already got it covered. If your practice is not on such a high level, while you're still alive phowa is a good thing to practice in preparation for your inevitable death. The transference of consciousness is to be done only after we have used all available methods to prolong our life, when we see unmistakable signs of our approaching death. It's very important that we never transfer our consciousness before our elements begin to dissolve.

There are three types of phowa:

- The highest form is dharmakaya phowa, which is a meditation on the Great Perfection. When you do Dzogchen meditation, there's no need to transfer anything because there's nothing to transfer, no place to transfer it, nor anyone to do it. That's the highest and greatest phowa practice.
- The second form is sambhogakaya phowa. This involves seeing everything as the mandala of the peaceful and wrathful deities. As it says in the Zhitro sadhana:

All phenomena appear as the mandala of the peaceful and
wrathful deities. These deities dissolve like a rainbow in
the sky.

Relax the mind in the natural state, which is the union of
appearance and emptiness, free from complexities.
All sounds are the speech of the wrathful and peaceful
deities.
This emptiness sound dissolves like the dragon's voice of
thunder disappears in the sky.

This verse describes the completion stage practice. Learn to merge your mind with everything in the mandala and just be part of that as it is, relaxing in the true nature.

• The third form of transference practice is known as nirmanakaya phowa, which was practiced widely and openly in Tibet. Visualize Buddha Amitabha sitting directly above your head and yourself as Vajrayogini or Yeshe Tsogyal. In the center of your visualized form imagine your central channel as being hollow and blue. In your heart chakra visualize your consciousness fused with the wind element in the form of a light green *thigle*, or sphere of light. While maintaining this visualization, eject your consciousness up through your central channel and crown chakra all the way up into Buddha Amitabha's heart center. This requires imagining both yourself and Buddha Amitabha in the form of wisdom rainbow bodies. Do not perceive any of this as solid. Practice this again and again until signs appear.*

There are signs that occur when you are becoming accomplished in the practice of phowa. You get a sensation on the fontanel on top

---

*To become accomplished in phowa, the transference of consciousness at the time of death, you need to practice it again and again while alive. You may have many lists of things to do, but keep this practice as one of them. Do it for one week or every few days. It's good to do it in a group, but doing it individually is good as well. During the dying process it is usually much more difficult to visualize or maintain a stable awareness, which is why practicing while you are in good health is important. Then when you're dying it will be easier to complete the practice successfully. You can also arrange for other people who are accomplished in phowa to do it either with you or for you during the dying process, when your elements are dissolving, and even after you've died.

Nirmanakaya phowa practice. Visualize Amitabha
above your crown and yourself as the dakini
Yeshe Tsogyal.

Line drawing by Andrea Nerozzi

of your head of throbbing, pulsing, or tingling. It can become sore or
itchy to the touch. Or maybe you get a headache in that area or feel
nauseous. Another sign is that drops of lymph bubble up at this spot
on top of the head. Lymph is a clear, fluidlike water, or it could be
more like dew. Some kind of moisture may appear—it could even be
a small bit of blood. A further sign is that the fontanel opens wide

enough to stick a blade of grass into it. (For a detailed discussion about the signs of successfully accomplishing the transference of consciousness, see chapter 20 of *The Essential Journey of Life and Death, Volume 2: Using Dream Yoga and Phowa as the Path.*)

Transfer the unborn self-awareness into the openness of space.

This is another reference to dharmakaya phowa. In this case, there's nothing to visualize—just continue abiding in unborn awareness.

When we are about to leave this body composed of flesh and blood,
Realize that it is impermanent and illusory.

In these two lines, Guru Padmasambhava emphasizes freedom from grasping. We habitually cling to our body and attach to the notion of a separate self. This body of flesh and blood is on loan from the five elements. It is compounded and fragile—an impermanent, magical mirage. Why do we cling to it? What are we holding on to? If we're still clinging, we don't understand the real situation.

In the case of sudden death, concentrate your mind in meditation and visualize your yidam, or personal meditational deity, to help balance the shock of the transition. Actually, whenever you experience disturbing situations it's best to maintain your mind in meditation. Relax into the primordial nature and don't give in to panic. Concentrate on your yidam deity, feel the presence of the Buddha and Guru Padmasambhava, or simply meditate on the true nature without thought. In the Dzogchen teachings we're told to visualize the deities arising instantly like a rainbow in the sky or like a fish jumping out of water. These are examples of visualizations where you immediately invoke the entire form of a divine being for a short time.

The stages of elemental dissolution during death are usually so quick that there is not much time to develop a visualization in different steps. This is because our faculties are decomposing and becoming increasingly dysfunctional. That's why it's important to meditate and develop your practice now, while you're still in good health.

When you experience the signs of approaching death, let go of all attachment and anger. Maintain equanimity, whether it's yourself or for another person who is dying. Try to create a peaceful environment and harmonious conditions. If it's another person who is dying, don't force anything on them. If they don't believe in the Dharma, allow them to die in that state of disbelief. If they do believe in the Dharma, help create an appropriate space in which to practice. Do whatever is suitable. The best way to support and benefit a dying person is with love and compassion. Above all, help them die peacefully. This is a crucial transition point, and if we let them get confused, it could mess them up, even if they were good practitioners.

There are situations where the dying person really believes in the Dharma although their relatives and friends do not. In that case we should not force any issues. We should just try to support a peaceful environment. If we begin to perform some Dharma activities for the dying person and their family members and friends don't appreciate it, it could cause a big scene. This would be a great obstacle to realization and hard on the dying person. This is not necessary. Instead, we should indirectly honor the Dharma and create a meditative atmosphere for that practitioner. Support them in simple ways, like offering to raise their pillows. Find ways to serve in the spirit of love and compassion. Inwardly meditate on Guru Padmasambhava, Vajrasattva, or Buddha Amitabha. Recite some mantras quietly and invoke the presence of the Dharma through your being. If you have the opportunity, right before the dissolving stages, you can move their body, adjusting their pillow to help them assume an upward, not-quite-sitting posture. If that's not possible, then try to get them into the lion's posture.

When the wind element dissolves into consciousness and consciousness is leaving the body, lightly touch the dying person on the top of their head, creating a little sensation around the crown chakra; you can even tug on some of their hairs. This can make a big difference, because when the consciousness leaves the body of an ordinary person it will leave through any opening that is available. The body has nine holes, but leaving through the central channel is always best because it provides a very neutral trajectory, free of anger and attachment. If they can somehow manage to exit through the top of the central channel, even nonpractitioners will make smoother transitions that will help them go to higher states of rebirth. Leaving from the lower parts of the body increases the likelihood of rebirth in the lower realms.

Most of the time a person's consciousness won't stay around too long. On average it will be gone after three days, which is why in Tibet they keep the corpse in the house for at least three and a half days. So it's good to occasionally pat the top of someone's head after their breathing has stopped, to direct their consciousness to that exit. If it looks strange to others who are in the room, just touch them gently on the crown and hold your hand there for a moment. Avoid causing any sensations in the lower parts of the body such as by holding the feet.

In a good Dharma environment you can discern the external signs and indicate the current phase of the process to the dying person. If he or she is a practitioner and no one is going to react negatively, then a close sangha member, friend, or relative can explain that this is the part of the process when consciousness leaves the body. Remind them to let go of all attachment and ego-clinging. In Tibet it is customary to read the Bardo Thodrol, or "Liberation through Hearing in the Bardo," commonly known in the West as The Tibetan Book of the Dead, very slowly and gently at the bedside of someone who is dying.* Chant it with great honor and respect, in a calm and gentle voice. This will help them recognize the signs and remember their practice. Support the mood of meditation, devotion, and faith. Even if the dying practitioner has already learned to recognize the signs, you can still be of help by simply recounting them. It's especially helpful to point out some of the main transitions, such as the descent of the white element and the ascent of the red element, and most importantly, to remind them to concentrate undistractedly and merge with the clear light. To say all this in a calm and peaceful tone is very beneficial.

---

*This is especially helpful since hearing is the last sense to stop working.

This is also a good time for sangha members to pray together. Recite Vajrasattva's hundred-syllable mantra, meant to purify defilements, and make offerings to the buddhas. Meditate and make everything very calm and peaceful, keeping unnecessary sounds to a minimum. Recite softly and practice in support of the dying person. A focused meditation on bodhichitta will truly put the power and blessings of the Buddha into the ceremony and positively affect the bardo voyager's mental state, even if he or she is not a practitioner. It will help them be confident and brave and orient them toward the purelands.

SUBTLE SIGNS OF APPROACHING DEATH

In the Bardo Thodrol, Guru Padmasambhava explains all the subtle signs associated with approaching death. According to the Zhitro teachings, there are two types of death: natural karmic death and accidental death. Karmic death is like a candle—it burns for a certain number of hours until its time is up. This is an example of the span of karmic life. Whether we live for a hundred years or thirty years depends on our karma. Karmic force is powerful, but it also allows for other things to happen, including accidental death. A person's karma might give her or him a hundred-year lifespan, but an adventitious obstacle could suddenly appear like a gust of wind and instantly the candle of life is blown out even though it still had fifty years to burn.

There could be nonvirtuous actions performed in the present life that would hasten the coming of a natural karmic death, but that is not necessarily the result. Nonvirtuous actions may not bear any result during this lifetime. Actually, most adventitious obstacles are part of our unpaid karmic debt from previous lifetimes that has come due. They are not anomalies that happen at random—they always have causes.

One section of the Bardo Thodrol deals with how to tell the difference between a karmic death and an accidental death. According to Guru Padmasambhava, there will be clear indications. Another section deals with removing the obstacles associated with the signs of accidental death. These are divided into outer, inner, and secret signs.

One possible outer sign is a personality change. Someone who was basically calm and peaceful may suddenly become short-tempered, moody, and small-minded. This may be a sign of the coming transition. With other people you can look at their head and see that their aura or energy has decreased. The complexion becomes pale, certain marks appear on the body or face, the fingernails become dull, and the hair on the nape of the neck stands up even if you try to comb it down. When sneezing, there may be involuntary urination, or they might pass stool at the same time. Hearing and vision begin failing, and smell and taste no longer work very well. All of these outer signs indicate physical weaknesses and imbalances in the system.

Other signs appear in dreams, but generally they are not considered significant if you only dream of them once or twice. If you have any of these dreams regularly, though, this is a definite sign. In one dream you are completely naked and running downhill at the same time. Another one involves people trying to catch you and lots of hands attempting to grab and punish you. There are other dreams, such as wearing heavy black cloth, riding certain animals, or traveling in certain directions. In another dream, you're very calm but handcuffed, or discover you're inside a place with no doors, like an iron box, or you're always traveling through tunnels. You may dream that you're climbing a beautiful ladder that suddenly breaks, or that you have fallen into a big hole or are interrupted by a broken bridge. You may be with many people who have died, such as family members or friends. Dreams in the earlier and middle parts of the night tend to reflect habitual patterns based on memories. Early morning dreams often pertain to the future. If one of these dreams occurs repeatedly in the early morning, this is a symptom of mental or physical imbalance and is a definite long-term sign of approaching death.

If you feel you may not live very long, examine your life. Remember to conduct your inquiry in the spirit of bodhichitta, with the intention of gaining knowledge and making the best use of your time here so you can accomplish something meaningful for yourself as well as for all sentient beings.

Signs indicating the presence of life-threatening obstacles reflect our attachment to things in this world that act as a hindrance and interrupt the continuity of beneficial activities. To overcome these obstacles, Guru Padmasambhava tells us to begin by making offerings to develop a strong feeling of connection with the Three Roots: the guru, the yidam, and the dakinis and dharmapalas. Be very generous with your sangha. Prepare a Vajrayana feast, a tsok offering, for your vajra brothers and sisters, then expand your feelings of love and compassion outward to include all sentient beings. Be charitable to others whom you feel really need it, like homeless people. In the spirit of peace and love for all beings you can even offer something to an animal. Then proceed to investigate the signs.

Distant signs may appear three or even five years before death. These are inauspicious omens, but if you recognize them for what they are, it may be relatively easy to modify the course of events by changing certain attitudes and applying practices to alter the result associated with that sign. But when the final signs do appear, it is very difficult to change things. Once in a while it might happen, but in most cases the outcome of the appearance of final signs is irreversible. However, the possibilities implied by the longer-term indications usually can be changed relatively easily. Therefore, Guru Rinpoche gave extensive teachings on all of this.

Of course, the signs will not occur for everyone in exactly the same way. If we respond by taking up the appropriate remedies and things do not change, this is an indication of karmic duration, and there is nothing we can do to change it unless we transform our body into a rainbow body. In any case, we must renew our practice, stabilize our meditation, and prepare to approach this transition joyfully.

Guru Padmasambhava explains that these signs do not always foreshadow death. In some cases they may signify the presence of serious obstacles that could lead to death if ignored. If you see any of these signs in yourself, it is good to meditate and practice, particularly on Guru Padmasambhava or Buddha Amitabha, and to rebalance your life habits. There may be symptoms that your vital energy is decreasing and that your potential is degenerating. Daily practice and meditation will definitely help balance and revitalize your life force. On the external level, efforts to preserve the lives of others, such as giving money to charities or working in shelters or a hospice, are restorative. You can help protect animals or save the lives of animals, such as releasing fish, as an expression of bodhichitta. It is also good to improve washed-out roads and repair broken bridges. These are very auspicious activities that will prolong life.

In the fourteenth and fifteenth centuries there was a great ter-ton named Tangtong Gyalpo, an emanation of Guru Padmasambhava who lived for more than 125 years. He was known as the "Iron Bridge Builder." Tangtong Gyalpo built over 108 bridges throughout Tibet and was possibly the first person in the world to engineer massive iron bridges able to span big rivers. Throughout Tibet there are many statues

Tangtong Gyalpo, the Iron Bridge Builder

Padma Samye Ling gonpa murals

of him wearing a long beard and holding an iron chain in his right hand to symbolize the bridges. He used a special metal that never rusted. Even the Chinese government appreciated him because he was a practitioner who directly improved the lives of ordinary people.

SUMMARY OF THE BARDO OF DYING

Guru Padmasambhava said, "Never thinking death will come, we make long-term plans." Even happy families and good friends must eventually part. It's as if we are meeting in an airport and will soon have to go our separate ways. The signs of death should not cause us to be frightened, angry, or upset. Death is a natural process. Without it, there is no birth. The two create an ongoing cycle that continues until we reach enlightenment. Death can make it seem like we're losing everything. But actually, if we are mindful and have a good understanding of the true nature, we can obtain great spiritual benefits and approach full realization through this transition. Therefore, we should not be worried, sad, or upset about death.

Life and death are like two sides of a coin. They are as inevitable as the cycle of day and night. From the viewpoint of higher realization, death is the experience of the dharmakaya (truth body) and sambhogakaya (light body). The experience of life is a nirmanakaya (form body) display. From the nirmanakaya, we can enter into the sambhogakaya and the dharmakaya, so we should not be upset or hesitant around death. We should go forward with wisdom and joyfully engage the process.

Many practitioners in Tibet have recognized the signs of death approaching. When they understand that they're dying, they don't feel upset or sad, but invite all their friends and family members to come to their departure. A teacher will ask all his or her students to come together, and an accomplished practitioner will invite sangha members and friends to a big festival. They often perform a tsok ceremony as a farewell gift before they leave. With great joy they host the festival and then abandon their earthly form to enter the dharmakaya and sambhogakaya alone.

Death is another dimension of our existence that we can explore. You've been here for a while, but to stay forever would be boring. Sooner or later you're going to have a look at the other side of this life. Buddha Maitreya taught that for those who realize that appearances are the display of the true nature of mind, the cycle of life and death is like walking from park to park, strolling from garden to garden. There's nothing strange or fearful about it. How beautiful it is!

Buddha Shakyamuni taught extensively about the empty, interdependent nature of all experiences, such as in the Meditation on Absolute Wisdom: The Moment of Death Sutra (see pages 152–58). Reciting and contemplating these teachings throughout our life can greatly influence how we approach death when it's our time to depart.

Read the life stories of many of the great masters and you'll be amazed and astonished to see the simple, joyful way they approached death. The Fifteenth Karmapa was Khakyab Dorje (1871–1922), whose name means "Pervasive Sky." As he was about to die, he sang, "Now it's time for Khakyab Dorje to pervade the sky!" When Longchenpa arrived at Samye Monastery, he said to one of his students, "I'm going to die in this place." He wasn't sick or anything, but he called the shots. "I would be happy to die here rather than acquire a rainbow body somewhere else." He wrote the following:

> *The time has come to go; like a traveler, I must be on my*
> *way. My joy in dying has been well-earned: it is greater*
> *than all the wealth in the ocean a merchant may have*
> *won, or the godlike power of having conquered armies,*
> *or the bliss found in meditation. So I wait no longer,*
> *but go to sit firmly on my seat in the supreme bliss that*
> *knows no death.*

He continued teaching for about two or three weeks, and then one day he said to his students, "Now I'm going to enter the dharmakaya, so let us meditate together one last time." Then while sitting in meditation, he dissolved his mind into the primordial nature.

We should not be frightened, hesitant, or timid. These transitions are part of the process of our total development. If we don't allow change, we will never get new results or make any progress toward enlightenment. This particular change at the end of each life represents a great opportunity to gain realization. Your mind becomes very influential at this time. Your intentions during the moment of death have an extraordinary effect on your future direction. Even an expert archer can shoot poorly if he or she is distracted at the moment of the arrow's release. Similarly, you may be a good practitioner in this lifetime, but a moment's carelessness during the dying process can drastically affect your chance for recognition during the bardo and a subsequent good rebirth. Likewise, increased concentration continuing in a positive direction at this time will be of great benefit even if you were not such a good practitioner during your life.

Fifth Bardo of the Luminosity of the True Nature

The next stage is called the "bardo of the luminosity of the true nature." This is also known as the "bardo of the clear light" or the "bardo of dharmata." After the moment of death, when breathing has stopped and the gross elements have dissolved into the subtlest space of consciousness, we reawaken in the clear light of the dharmakaya. Most ordinary beings with no spiritual knowledge or exposure to bardo teachings will not recognize what is happening at this point, and it will last only a short time. There's no fixed duration for the amount of time you will spend in any of these phases. Various factors such as the condition of the channels and the manner of death determine just how the changes proceed. But even if the vision is fleeting and only lasts a moment, a good practitioner can recognize and expand on that flash and gain enlightenment in the dharmakaya.

If we recognize the clear light at that time, the confusion of the bardos comes to an end. This is the best opportunity for enlightenment in the dharmakaya. But if we're unable to recognize the nature of mind, the energy of our awareness will begin to express itself. From here, liberation becomes progressively harder. The eighty emotions that were momentarily inactivated gradually return. Because we have not yet recognized and merged with our clear light awareness, this bardo begins with an experience of awesome sounds, very bright lights, and then tiny beams of light. The sounds and lights that are experienced at this time do not exist externally. They are all emanations of our own primordial nature, appearing in forms that you have to recognize for what they truly are.

During the final moments of the bardo of the moment of death we had a chance to gain enlightenment at the level of the dharmakaya. If this does not happen, we enter the bardo of luminosity, where there is a chance to become enlightened in the sambhogakaya. If you are familiar with the Dzogchen practice of *togal*, the "leaping over" practice that uses meditations involving light and color, you are prepared for transcendent recognition and liberation in the sambhogakaya.

The visions that arise at this point are not created by anyone, nor are they a reflection of conditioned habitual energy. They arise spontaneously from the true nature, the domain of primordial wisdom, and appear to consciousness under certain conditions. According to the Dzogchen teachings, these colors and lights are natural qualities of our primordial wisdom. They are both visions of our intrinsic nature as well as the basis of all the sounds and colors perceived during our lifetime. At this time we're really experiencing all of them effortlessly, at full intensity, unobscured by the poisons. If we're able to recognize the true nature of these appearances and merge our awareness with this luminous display, we have an opportunity to gain enlightenment in the sambhogakaya.

First comes the experience of sound, which is known as *chonyid rangdra* in Tibetan, the "voice of the true nature" or the "echo of primordial wisdom." This sound is not soft and nice. It's much louder and stronger than heavy metal music. Guru Padmasambhava compared it to the sound of a thousand thunders or the destruction of the universe. It's a very big noise! But again, this awesome turbulence is not happening externally—it is an echo of the primordial nature. If you can recognize it as the reverberation of transcendent wisdom and not react negatively, you can put an end to the bardo process. If we recognize that the sounds we experience in the bardo of the true nature are actually the natural expressions of our own awareness, we will instantly be liberated from the suffering caused by mistakenly believing that they're outside of us. If you don't recognize these sounds for what they are, things get a bit harder. The earlier experiences are relatively gentle and peaceful. As you continue, the waves get a little rougher, like whitewater rafting in the Rocky Mountains.

If you're frightened by the sounds and miss the opportunity for recognition, concentrate in preparation for the next visions, which involve very powerful blazing lights that appear in front of you. This is called *chonyid rango* in Tibetan, or "recognizing the self-arising nature." Guru Padmasambhava says that this light is stronger than a thousand suns. It shines so brightly it feels like it's going to pierce right through you, like a shower of powerful arrows.

This is followed by a vision of tiny five-colored beams of light, which is called *chonyid rangzer* in Tibetan, or "self-emanating light of the nature." The sounds may be irritating or frightening. You may get upset or angry and start running to escape, but the sounds and the beams of light pursue you. You desperately want to get away, and all your hopes and fears begin to arise very strongly. This same distress may continue when you experience the lights of the peaceful and wrathful deities. If you begin to cherish an attachment or become frightened, clinging to false discriminations, you will only be trapped in more confusion.

The opportunity for liberation here is still wide open for determined practitioners. When hearing the sounds, recognize the voice of the true nature as what you were practicing during your lifetime when you recited mantra. The brilliant lights are perceived while alive through togal practice.* When yogis and yoginis experience these things after death, their recognition is perfect because they've seen it before. They don't feel scared, but quite naturally understand. They merge with the true nature of these visions and are easily liberated. If you don't recognize the lights and sounds, the next phase begins with many distinctly colored bright lights that arise one after another. These signal the appearance of the Dhyani Buddhas.† Along with each bright light, a very dull light glows nearby. Ordinary beings who are afraid of the bright lights will feel attracted to

---

*Togal is an advanced Dzogchen practice that one must train in directly with an accomplished master. (See the glossary for a general description of togal.)
†Dhyani Buddhas are primordial celestial buddhas that have always existed since the beginning of time; each is represented by a color, a direction, and one of the five elements. These represent the five buddha families so the terms are interchangeable. (See the glossary for more on the Dhyani Buddhas).

the duller light. This dull light is the essence of negative emotions and karmic attachments. Your ignorance is being put to the test, and the tendency to grasp phenomena is rekindled.

When the sounds, lights, and rays first appear during the bardo of luminosity, your mind is still relatively lucid. But now subtle obscurations and negative emotions such as anger, attachment, and jealousy begin to reappear in a more active form. People who don't have any practical experience of the Dharma will tend to react at this point. It's quite common for a recently deceased person to feel as though they are still associated with their old body and not understand that they're actually dead. It feels like a dream. This initiates a new phase of detailed displays and reactivates one's previous underlying tendencies to further confuse the situation.

In compassionate response to this mistaken notion of embodiment, visions of various buddhas arise. This is the second opportunity for liberation through recognition of the visions of the Dhyani Buddhas, as described in The Tibetan Book of the Dead. First, the peaceful buddhas will appear, beginning with the five buddha families as represented by the Dhyani Buddhas.*

---

*The Dhyani Buddhas are always grouped with their consorts, representing the tantric principles of the Vajrayana. Thus the union of male and female buddhas from each of the five buddha families represents five aspects of enlightened mind and the five qualities of the buddha nature that are inherent in all beings. Each Dhyani Buddha is associated with a specific color, element, symbol, and direction, depicting the natural inseparability of relative and absolute truth, form and emptiness, appearance and awareness, and skillful means and wisdom. These polarities only *seem* to be at odds from the perspective of duality mind; in fact, they are always together. Visualizing each of the Buddha families empowers us to directly experience the flexible, empty nature of all appearances. In addition to expressing the truth of the union of seeming opposites, the Dhyani Buddhas are also associated with healing specific physical, emotional, and psychological ailments. As well, each Dhyani Buddha is associated with a particular negative state of mind and has the power to transform that state into its innate wisdom essence.

The Buddha families are depicted as follows: Vairochana and Mamaki represent the Buddha family and are at the center of the four directions and are usually blue. The Dhyani Buddhas of the east are Vajrasattva-Akshobhya and Dhatvishvari, who are white and represent the Vajra family. The Dhyani Buddhas of the south are Ratnasambhava and Lochana, who are yellow and represent the Ratna family. The Dhyani Buddhas of the west are Amitabha and Pandaravasini, who are red and represent the Padma family. The Dhyani Buddhas of the north are Amoghasiddhi and Tara, who are green and represent the Karma family.

The primoridial buddhas Samantabhadra and
Samanthabhadri in union

Padma Samye Ling

A skylike expanse of great blue light is projected out from your heart center just before the appearance of the buddha forms. This is the light of the dharmadhatu (i.e., absolute) wisdom. At first it is apparent that the light is emanating from you, but when the buddhas appear it's as if they were separate from you. In the center of this radiant blue field you will see a small circle of white light. (If you've received more advanced training under the auspices of a qualified lama, this is the same light referred to in togal practice.) If you're able to recognize it, you'll see that this light is none other than Samantabhadra and Samantabhadri* in union, and you'll attain enlightenment immediately, without further bardo experiences.

---

*Samantabhadra and Samantabhadri are primoridal male and female buddhas who symbolize the natural inseparability of appearance and emptiness.

Vairochana, one of the Five Dhyani Buddhas,
and consort Mamaki
Padma Samye Ling

If you don't recognize this, the white light expands to encompass your entire visual space. If you're well-acquainted with the practice of visualizing the buddhas of the Vajra family, you will easily recognize Buddha Vairochana and his consort, Mamaki, sitting in the center of this white field. If you understand even for a second that this vision is an emanation of primordial wisdom inseparable from your natural mind, you'll completely change your karmic momentum and attain enlightenment in the presence of Buddha Vairochana.

If you fail to recognize Buddha Vairochana as a display of your own primordial wisdom and instead experience a subject-object duality between yourself and what appears, another white light emerges. This presents the next opportunity for recognition that is described as "white lights following one after another like clouds." It's also known as the "light of Vajrasattva" and is associated with mirrorlike wisdom.

Vajrasattva, a buddha associated with purification,
and consort Dhatvishvari

Padma Samye Ling

If you recognize this as the radiance of your own mind, your confusion will end and there will be no more bardos. From the center of this brilliant white light, Buddha Vajrasattva and his consort, Dhatvishvari, appear surrounded by a refuge tree.* This entire display emanates from your own heart center.

The next phase begins with a golden-yellow light. Nondual recognition of this light as the wisdom of equanimity leads to enlightenment in the sambhogakaya. To welcome you, Buddha Ratnasambhava, his consort Buddhalochana, and their refuge tree will appear from the midst of that radiance, and you can be liberated without further wandering.

---

*Each school of Tibetan Buddhist has its own refuge tree, consisting of the buddhas invoked by the lineage and the masters of the lineage, as well as dakinis, protectors, and so on, which are visualized in meditation.

Ratnasambhava, one of the Five Dhyani Buddhas,
and consort Buddhalochana

Padma Samye Ling

This is followed by a deep red light that pervades the whole of space. This is the radiance of discriminating wisdom. If you have practiced with Amitabha, the Buddha of Infinite Light, you can easily recognize this light and break the cycle of karmic rebirth. Resplendent in sambhogakaya display, Buddha Amitabha and his consort, Pandaravasini, will appear, surrounded by their refuge tree.

Subsequently, an intensely green light radiates. This is the light of all-accomplishing wisdom. Having practiced with the deities of the karma family will allow you to recognize the nature of this display. If you have a clear understanding of this vision, you can be immediately enlightened. From the center of that green field, Buddha Amoghasiddhi and Samayatara will appear in union on the central lotus of a cosmic refuge tree.

Amitabha, celestial buddha of the purelands,
and consort Pandaravasini
Padma Samye Ling

Samantabhadra and Samantabhadri, or Vajrasattva and his consort, Dhatvishvari, abide in the center of the mandala and are the main deities related to the Zhitro teachings. The five other Dhyani Buddhas with their consorts, together with various bodhisattvas associated with each buddha family, arise as their retinue. Altogether, these make up the forty-two peaceful deities, which are followed by the appearance of the fifty-eight wrathful deities. This is the mandala of the Guhyagarbha Tantra. All of these buddhas are the display of original wisdom that structures each person's body and mind.

Through the inspiration of these teachings, begin to investigate the subtle dimensions of the world and you will discover that the whole mandala appears within you. There is nothing outside of you. On the basis of this understanding, practice and meditate so that when the time comes to die you will recognize all of these visions as your own projections and blissfully merge with the true nature of your mind, the source of everything.

Amoghasiddhi, one of the Five Dhyani Buddhas,
and consort Samayatara
Padma Samye Ling

It will be of immense benefit during the bardo of luminosity if now, while you are still alive, you regularly practice visualizing these deities and reciting their mantras. If you have a good practice, you already know that these visions are expressions of mind that arise as the energy of pure love, compassion, and wisdom. This is what the Dhyani Buddhas and their retinues represent. If you're familiar with this kind of meditation, you have a good chance of attaining enlightenment. You don't have to introduce yourself to your own mother. If you recognize any one of these buddhas during this bardo, you will be enlightened. When this happens, all of your bardo experiences will stop—it's all over in one moment of recognition. The entire "external" cosmos will dissolve within you, and then instead of being defined by the limitations of karmic rebirth, you can go anywhere and take any form. You get a pass to the red carpet club, while those who aren't familiar with these visions wander around awhile in a very busy place that looks something like Calcutta!

If we somehow overlook all of these opportunities for liberation by not recognizing the peaceful buddhas, we'll be subject to the onset of what are known as the wrathful buddhas,* and from there it gets even tougher. Not only is there the reappearance of the blinding radiance and intense beams of light that seem to shine right through us, but terrifying thunder resounds and a thousand fires burn as the wrathful buddhas arise.

The Zhitro sadhana text "Self-Liberated Mind" reads:

> *The unimpeded skill of their radiance*
> *Arises in the conchlike mansion . . .*

The "conchlike mansion" refers to the brain. The channels projecting away from the brain represent the wrathful deities. We won't go into all of the details here, but presently most of the peaceful buddhas reside within the heart center, while some abide in other chakras and channels of the nervous system. Altogether these are the forty-two peaceful buddhas. In addition, fifty-eight wrathful buddhas reside within the conchlike mansion of the brain, or crown chakra. Altogether there are one hundred peaceful and wrathful deities.

You have probably seen wrathful buddhas in thangkas that have three eyes and many legs and arms, surrounded by an aura of fire. These kinds of forms will appear before you at this point in the bardo. All of these visions are nothing other than a display of your own primordial wisdom. If you are experienced in the visualization of the peaceful and wrathful deities, you will understand that these visions are inseparable from your own primordial wisdom. They are expressions of your buddha nature. Don't get in the habit of rejecting or running away from things that you don't immediately recognize, or nervously assume that you know what something is without inquiring. By recognizing these forms, you have another chance to merge with these visions and attain enlightenment.

---

*The "wrath" of these buddhas, who are actually teachers and protectors, is based entirely on love, compassion, and wisdom, not anger. Their terrifying appearances are used to immediately release destructive emotions and negative karmic behaviors into wisdom, which is their natural condition before dualistic consciousness distorts their arising energy. The power of their appearance corresponds to the density of negative karmic patterns that are being skillfully purified.

The peaceful deities

Painting by Sergey Noskov

The wrathful deities

Painting by Sergey Noskov

Buddha with snake head
Vajrakilaya and Medicine Buddha Temple, Padma Samye Ling

In Tibet there was a thangka painter who was working on a painting of the hundred peaceful and wrathful deities. His young daughter was always by his side, but she didn't pay too much attention to his art until he painted a certain wrathful buddha whose head was a snake.

The little girl had a strong reaction to this image and asked her father, "What is this strange-looking creature?" "This is nothing to feel strange about," the father said. "This is one of the many forms of the Buddha. All these figures are buddhas." Then she asked, "Where are these buddhas now?" He explained, "While you are alive, you might not be able to see these buddhas. But when you die they will come and show themselves. This buddha with a snake's head is the last among all the buddhas that you will experience at that time. When you see this form, don't be deluded into thinking that you haven't died."

This snake-headed buddha made a very big impression in the little girl's mind. She would remember his form and how her father said it was important to remember that she would see the Buddha in this form after death. Throughout her life, this thought was in her mind, again and again. After she died, she went through all the bardo experiences but didn't recognize what was happening until she saw the final snake-headed buddha. At that moment she remembered, "Oh! Here is the vision of the Buddha my father told me about. This is my own mind's projection in the bardo. It doesn't exist externally, so I shouldn't react and create more karma." Simply remembering this helped her relax and stopped her from drifting into a more deluded, confused state. She actually enjoyed a good realization due to this understanding.

The wrathful buddhas emanate from our crown chakra, accompanied by a violent eruption of light and sound. Visualization is extremely clear during this time. Everything is coming on strong. If you meditate well and know the importance of concentration, you have another opportunity to recognize that all this is a projection of your own mind—a display of primordial wisdom. Knowing this, all further stages become unnecessary and you can rest in your mother's lap.

All the peaceful and wrathful deities are nothing other than a reflection of your own primordial wisdom. They are emanations of your own mind and do not exist in and of themselves. They are like just another display of the dream state. As you experience these deities, you're actually traveling in a deeper dimension of the dream world.

Let's look at the text to summarize:

> *When the bardo of intrinsic reality is dawning upon me,*
> *Abandoning all terror and fear . . .*

This bardo begins with the most intense experience of the primordial luminosity of clear light awareness. Because we usually cling to hopes and fears, Guru Padmasambhava urges us not to be timid or afraid at this time. We need to know that whatever arises is the self-radiant energy of the mind and does not contain even a single atom of objective reality. The entire experience is contained in our own mind, just like a dream. Understanding this crucial point leads to liberation.

Whether it's peaceful or wrathful,

> *recognize that whatever arises is the self-appearance of*
> *awareness.*

Everything we see is a display of primordial wisdom—the lighting up of the true nature. Why should we be frightened by our own mind? Perhaps we're a bit apprehensive and afraid when we consider what it will be like to experience the clear light of our true nature. But Guru Padmasambhava and the Buddha both taught us to regard birth and death as mere thoughts and dualistic concepts.

> *Realize it as the apparitions of the intermediate state.*

The bardo of the luminosity of the true nature actually consists of two stages. At first you are completely trapped between the red and white elements and everything goes black, like during the night of a new moon. Then you have a vision of the true nature that is unimpeded, completely transparent, beyond conceptions, uncompounded, and free from complexities. In Dzogchen this is called the "primordially pure vision of trekcho."* This is the emptiness aspect of the true nature coemergent with the clear light luminosity, and you will experience it at this time in the bardo. You are one with the condition of primordial purity—the state of the true nature. Merging your awareness with this reality the moment it arises resolves everything into "one taste." This is known as "the child merging with the mother clear light." In this way you become enlightened in the dharmakaya.

---

*Trekcho, a more advanced Vajrayana practice, is an extraordinary technique used to immediately discover the enlightened nature of the mind through the blessings of your personal teacher and lineage. During the bardo of the luminosity of the true nature, this same nature of mind is naturally revealed for every being undergoing this process.

From the moment the secret signs appear during the dissolution of the elements, to the first glimpse of the true nature, and through the subsequent experiences of the sounds, lights, and rays as well as the visions of the hundred peaceful and wrathful deities, everything is a manifestation of the bardo of the luminosity of the true nature. Whether you recognize during the descent of the white light, the ascent of the red light, or through one of the visions of the Zhitro deities, all are forms of liberation in the bardo of luminosity that lead directly to enlightenment in the sambhogakaya or nirmanakaya. If you practiced at all while you were alive, you can realize accomplishments during this bardo that may have seemed completely beyond your capacities when you were alive.

This bardo features many different visions, one after another, so there are endless opportunities to become enlightened. The continuity of primordial experience embodied in these visions is known as the "lamps" in togal practice. Here we see the very same hues, rainbows, rays, and also what are called "vajra chains of light." These represent the activity of transcendental wisdom that arises spontaneously as sounds, colors, and shapes in motion. Without meditating or visualizing anything, the visions we've been cultivating in our practice appear before us now in all of their intensity. To awaken during this display is known as "enlightenment in the form body." All of these visions are part of the bardo of the clear light, the luminosity aspect of the true nature.

Sixth Bardo of Becoming

After moving through the transitions of the first five bardos, your consciousness is now heading toward its next karmically driven embodiment. This is the bardo of becoming. Guru Padmasambhava also refers to it as the bardo of karmic possibilities. This stage lasts from the end of the visions of the peaceful and wrathful deities until we take a new birth.

This bardo is known as the time of the six uncertainties: (1) There is still no certain place to settle. You only seem to be able to find marginal shelter, under trees or between rocks. Often you are in wide-open spaces that offer no refuge. (2) You're not sure what you're doing. Change is the only certainty. There's no continuity. You might become involved with something, and then it totally changes, just as in dreams. (3) The source of your food is uncertain unless someone dedicates it to you through meditation and mantra recitation. (4) The moods and concerns of friends are also uncertain, as are your own visions and "views." (5) The focus of your awareness and (6) your very identity are also uncertain.

Generally, the entire bardo experience lasts no longer than forty-nine days, but that's just an average. The fourth and fifth bardos, including the arising of the awesome sounds, lights, and five-colored rays, as well as the visions of peaceful and wrathful deities, can all be experienced in as few as three days. It depends on the person. Seven weeks is an average. Guru Padmasambhava said that the luminosity bardo is usually completed within two or three weeks, and that the rest of the time we move toward rebirth in the bardo of becoming, as our habit patterns gradually develop toward a new birth and life.

Some people experience these transitions very quickly. Others may stay in the bardo for years because their karma is conditioned by strong ego-clinging, heavy attachments, and powerful anger. But generally the bardo experience averages about seven weeks. That's why Tibetans consider these forty-nine days to be so very important.

When we were young boys in Tibet, people would often leave a person's body in place for forty-nine days after their death. Of course our legal system allowed for this. Tibet used to be a very independent and free country with its own ways. After seven weeks they would take the body outside and offer it to vultures in what is known as a "sky burial." Many lamas insisted on this in place of cremation or earth burial, so that their death was of direct benefit to sentient beings.

The process of rebirth is a complex situation where many things can happen, so it's quite common for Tibetans to perform ceremonies for the dead on each of the forty-nine days, meditating on love and compassion, and generating bodhichitta on behalf of the deceased person. Since everything is uncertain for someone after they die, these blessings help them be mindful and have a positive influence on their transmigration.

Even if the deceased was an accomplished practitioner and has already taken birth, it's still good to do these prayers and offer them encouragement. Mantra recitation and generosity practices are both very important. The Seven Line Prayer, the Vajra Guru mantra, Tara's mantra, and the hundred syllable mantra of Vajrasattva will all remind them of their meditation practice and help them apply themselves more fervently in the moment. At the end of each session, dedicate the merit to them by name. This is a great support and has an immediate influence on the impressionable mental body of someone moving through the bardos after death.

There are special prayers you may want to recite from The Tibetan Book of the Dead that invoke all the buddhas and bodhisattvas to guide and assist the bardo voyager. The dedication of food to the deceased is done in every school of Buddhism. Generous offerings are also made to sangha members, and the resultant merit is dedicated to individual beings. In the Vajrayana we perform special ceremonies called *sur* offerings, which invoke Avalokiteshvara, the Buddha of Compassion. We meditate and make offerings of fire and smoke. Water offerings and tormas are also used in these rituals. These practices are usually done for forty-nine days after someone dies.

There are practitioners who do these practices all the time, even when no one they know has died, because there are always many beings wandering through the bardo, including this very moment. Even if they're not practitioners, to dedicate the merit gained through acts of kindness and generosity is definitely of great benefit to beings in the bardo.

When highly realized beings die, their consciousness is ejected up through their central channel and out the top of their head via the wisdom wind. In ordinary beings, karmic winds drive consciousness out through any part of the body *except* the central channel. Ordinary beings subject to dualistic confusion commonly experience the familiar reality they lived during their lifetimes. The Buddha's Abhidharma teachings and the Dzogchen Self-Arising Primordial Awareness Tantra both state that if you're not able to recognize the clear light, your habitual patterns reactivate, and the corresponding visions can remain very vivid for about two and a half weeks or even a little longer.

Because thoughts are extremely powerful in determining experience, beings in the sixth bardo have full-blown hallucinations. If we don't recognize what has happened, we just continue distracting ourselves as we've always done. During this time we will have experiences identical to what we typically saw and heard during our lives. We'll dress as we used to and busy ourselves in familiar ways. We may wander around the house or the places where we used to work. Our psycho-physical habits are still powerful.

At this point in the bardo, the transparent mental body that we identify with is filled with feelings and sense consciousnesses, although our perceptions and experiences are very unstable, similar to when we dream at night. The only ones who can see the mental body are those who are in the same situation, or highly developed beings with wisdom eyes. After two and a half weeks, most of these visions will have subsided.

It helps to have been practicing meditation and mindfulness during your life, because in the bardo, the moment you think of something, it manifests. There's no effort required for this to happen. Thoughts become extremely powerful, and your mind is almost entirely controlled by its habit patterns. While alive, we're so engrossed with our physical body and shielded by layers of karmic involvement that we don't see such immediate effects. But in the bardo, although dualistic conceptions can still operate, certain psycho-physical barriers and limitations are completely gone.

At this time, the continual wandering of your mental body may become tiresome, and you may start to have some doubts that your practice will ever lead to a higher rebirth or to the purelands. Do not be discouraged. Devoted practitioners can still have a liberating insight at this time and completely change their direction.

The mind is very powerful now—whatever you imagine will happen immediately. If you recite the Seven Line Prayer three times, chant

The Fifth Dalai Lama
Padma Samye Ling gonpa murals

the Vajra Guru mantra, and visualize Guru Padmasambhava, he will definitely be with you. Any or all of the buddhas will appear the instant they are invoked. Thought is so powerful at this point that the mind is immediately and profoundly transported into the context of its mental events. If you can take advantage of this, it can serve as a great support for a successful transmigration.

A deeply devoted practitioner is never separate from the guru. In fact, it is said that the guru takes up residence on their doorstep. In the seventeenth century, the great Fifth Dalai Lama became king of Tibet, and although outwardly he belonged to the Gelugpa school— one of the four schools of Tibetan Buddhism, the others being the Nyingma, Kagyu, and Sakya—his inner practice had strong roots in the Nyingma tradition. He was also a great terton. A well-known *geshe* (a Buddhist scholar, similar to a PhD) named Dago Ramjam was his good friend. One day, Dago Ramjam arrived and tried to climb into the Dalai Lama's room through a window. The Dalai Lama asked him why he didn't use the door, and Dago Ramjam replied, "I know that Guru Padmasambhava sits on your threshold—I didn't want to crush him."

In the Mahayana sutras, Buddha Shakyamuni said, "Whenever any-one thinks of me, I am immediately present right in front of them." At this point in the bardo, this is not only true of the Buddha—if you focus on anyone with true love and compassion, your experience will instantly change. Simply meditating on the true nature for one moment transforms everything. This is why it's extremely important to train our minds in love and compassion. Whenever you are faced with a difficult situation, if you can simply relax your mind, settle into meditation, and reconnect with pure love and the presence of Guru Padmasambhava, you are developing a very important skill. In this way the more fright-ening bardo experiences will remind you to return to the primordial source and merge your mind with Guru Padmasambhava, Vajrasattva, or any of the buddhas. All of the terrifying noises and uncomfortable visions are related to the winds. If you learn about these phenomena now, the bardo experiences will be just like a fire alarm going off, and you will remember precisely what you need to do.

Bardo beings can move freely in any direction without encountering obstacles. The Buddha taught that the mental body can only be stopped by two things: entry into the womb of a female with whom you share a karmic connection for conception; and the diamond seat at Bodhgaya, India, known as *Dorje Den* in Tibetan, or *Vajra Asana* in Sanskrit, where there is a powerful double dorje directly under the spot where Buddha Shakyamuni attained enlightenment. This special place in Bodhgaya, as well as your future mother's womb, cannot be accessed by your mental body at this point in the bardo. Other than that, you're free to go anywhere. The mental body has no visa or immigration problems, and travel is extremely quick. Maybe you'll fly to Tibet, circle it three times, and zip back to America. However, everything is a little uncomfortable because it's so unstable.

At this point, bardo voyagers are restless, and their uncomfortable feelings gradually increase. This continues for about two weeks. You don't like who you are or your circumstances, even though you may not recognize your real situation. For an ordinary person, the speed and uncontrollable chaos is overwhelming. Fear and anxiety may begin to dominate their mood. There are no gross elements present at this stage. The bardo consciousness is developing in relation to its karmic winds of the four elements of earth, water, fire, and air. These four winds interact with our habit patterns and emotional instability and give rise to further visions that tend to be rather frightening. When the earth wind becomes unbalanced, it causes you to feel like there are landslides and earthquakes. As the water wind is affected, you get stormy visions of heavy rain and crashing waves, as if there were a hurricane, and this makes your consciousness more unsteady. When the fire wind is influenced, you see houses, buildings, and whole cities burning, and great fires spreading through mountain forests. When the wind of air is affected, you feel intense pressure and hear howling and rumbling, as if a tornado is approaching.

If you were a kindhearted, loving person, a guide often appears to assist you through this phase. This is very helpful because the situation is beginning to seem exhausting and endless, even as new changes continue to develop rapidly. For those who have been involved in negative activities like torture, killing humans, or even butchering animals, malicious beings appear who cause trouble and confusion for them wherever they go. Anytime they begin to feel safe and secure, someone suddenly appears to disturb them and destroy their peace of mind. This happens over and over again.

According to the Vajrayana, the sun and moon are directly connected to the red and white elements that cause our usual experience of day and night. But at this point in the bardo these two elements have already separated and disintegrated, and without them we don't experience night or day. During this part of the journey, the environment appears in a dim twilight.

After about three weeks, the habit patterns of your previous life begin to lose force and dissolve. The energy of the patterns begins to wane, and your normal vision of things is shown to be false. At this point your consciousness undergoes a crisis of deep uncertainty about the nature of existence. Everyone who wanders this far into the bardo will have this kind of experience, regardless of their habits. Gradually, visions of your future life appear like the glow before sunrise. This gets stronger and clearer as you approach the dawn of future habit patterns and karmic rebirth. It's not yet very bright, but even so, it's attractive because you're tired of being afraid and wandering without any support. During the fourth week, the emerging pattern of the future becomes even stronger. You start to feel comfortable with it. Your association with your previous habitual body ends as a new form arises, and you like the feel of the energy. It's like taking birth in the god realm, with a rosy anticipation of some security as the light slowly increases.

While the beginning of your next life is inevitably approaching, lights of different colors and intensities will appear. The nature of your thoughts and attachments determines which color is attractive and where you will take rebirth. By the seventh week you abandon almost all attention to past memories and shift your focus to your new situation. Everything becomes increasingly defined until somewhere around forty-nine days, when the average person takes up residence in a womb.

In most cases, reincarnation is not a conscious decision—it's determined by the power of karma. If you haven't practiced, you will have difficulty recognizing the opportunities for liberation in the clear light, and you'll be carried by the force of your karmic winds. They will drive you along and you won't have much choice. Practitioners who have some understanding of the mind have the ability to influence their destination and choose a higher rebirth. They may even get to be born to parents they like. But most beings just wander awhile, visiting different places in their mental body. After an average of forty-nine days, they re-enter the bardo of birth and life in one of the six realms* according to their karma.

When consciousness begins to take rebirth, it is conceived in the same way that it left, between the two elements contributed by the parents—the red element from the mother and the white element from the father. During conception, consciousness is again trapped between the two elements, where it is relatively comfortable for a while. For human beings, this usually results in being born in a womb. Buddha described four ways of taking birth: (1) from a womb; (2) through an egg; (3) in the presence of moisture; and (4) miraculously, or instantaneously.

As Guru Padmasambhava said,

> *When the bardo of rebirth is dawning upon me,*
> *Holding one-pointedly to that single great wish . . .*

Concentrating your attention with devotion and spiritual inspiration is what really matters now. Maintaining a one-pointed mind is extremely important. You've heard many times that the mind is powerful—it's the engine for all our activities. But in this bardo the power of the mind is so great that if we have even a little devotion and inspiration we can stop being scattered and make significant progress toward accomplishing our goals.

---

*According to the Buddha, there are six realms in samsara where sentient beings wander, including the hell realm, hungry ghost realm, animal realm, human realm, antigod realm, and god realm.

Buddha Shakyamuni said, "Inspiration and devotion are the door to enlightenment." You must have them in order for practice and meditation to ripen into realization. Without them, we close the door to awakening. Inspiration and devotion connect what you learn with the energy of your heart. You may have memorized all the Buddha's teachings and be very educated and culturally sophisticated, but without inspired devotion this is just dry knowledge and will be of no help in the face of death. Even during your life you'll only touch the surface of the teachings and never come to a profound understanding of yourself.

If we read about the lives of greatly realized beings, we find that every one of them demonstrated three things: a single-pointed mind, inspired vision, and great devotion. These qualities led them to transcendent awakening. The great Dzogchen master and scholar Longchenpa claimed that his final realization was due to the inspiration of the lineage masters and devotion to his teachers. Look at the life of Milarepa, who had no monastic education. How did he attain enlightenment? He had tremendous devotion to his teacher, Marpa, cherishing Marpa's every word in his heart like drops of golden nectar. Marpa's teachings inspired him to attain buddhahood. By simply accepting his guru's every word as true, Milarepa was able to focus one-pointedly on that single great wish and become one of the most accomplished masters of Tibetan Buddhism.

Connect firmly with our former good karma.

Joyful effort creates the continuity that lies at the heart of spiritual growth. Therefore, joyfully reestablish a link with your good karma. Your bodhichitta motivation must be uninterrupted. Courage, joyful effort, commitment, and confidence are the essence of maintaining that connection. In Tibetan we say *leche trothud*, which means "firmly reconnecting with our stream of merit" so that our body, speech, and mind are continually united with the path.

In Tibet and India, farmers dig irrigation channels to bring water to their fields. They frequently clear out all the debris that collects in them so the water won't flow over the sides, but can continue on to the fields. Guru Padmasambhava used the example of renovating a broken channel to indicate how you should correct your understanding and try to ensure a reconnection with the Dharma in your future life.

The Vajrayana is replete with effective techniques to help us reconnect with our clarity. Having missed all of the previous opportunities, achieving realization in the sixth bardo is like linking one continuum with another so that the flow of virtue is uninterrupted across lives. By one-pointedly holding this single great wish, we secure our way, leading our consciousness directly to the heart of Buddha Amitabha in his nirmanakaya pureland.

The bardos have to be learned through diligent study and practice so that we become intimate with this territory—not just intellectually acquainted, but natural and skillful in our responsiveness. With practice we can definitely reach enlightenment either during or immediately after the moment of death. If we miss both of these opportunities, Guru Padmasambhava advises us to use the metaphor of repairing an irrigation channel as an illustration of how to reconnect with our former good karma, because our consciousness is looking to take rebirth.

Closing the womb door, remember to turn away.
It is the very time when courage and pure perception are needed.
Avoid jealousy and visualize our parents as father-mother guru.

Now is the time to renew your joyful efforts and prepare to take rebirth. The teachings explain that we still have many choices, which appear as different lights. Whenever dull lights loom before you, try to avoid them. If a light is bright and strong, go for it, even if it makes you feel a little uncomfortable. You're moving toward conception and rebirth and are in the process of choosing your parents. The more brilliant lights lead to good parents who are kind and supportive. The weak, dull glow may seem more easygoing and attractive but will turn out to be a poor choice. Ideally, the couple should be very spiritual, open, kind, compassionate, and intelligent; these are the best kind of parents to connect with. Courage, pure perception, and bodhichitta motivation are really needed now in order to avoid an inauspicious situation.

When you see these lights in the bardo of karmic possibilities, remember the instructions. If your consciousness is drawn toward the dreamy dull lights, muster all your strength and courage to pull yourself back from going in that direction. Remember the teachings and recognize the primordial nature of mind. If this is not possible, at least hold to pure perceptions and have good thoughts. This will turn you away from lower rebirths.

Consciousness is conceived through the perfect union of the red and white elements contributed by the mother and father. If the three humors of bile, wind, and phlegm are all in balance, consciousness will be bound up with the elements of conception. Immediately before you are about to be conceived you'll see your parents in union. If you're going to be a girl, you naturally develop two emotions: attachment to the father and jealousy toward the mother. If you are going to be a boy you'll attach to the mother and be jealous of the father. To avoid this reaction, meditate on your parents as the father and mother deities in

Guru Rinpoche and his consort, the dakini Yeshe Tsogyal

Personal thangka of Venerable Khenpo Rinpoches

union. Regard them as Vajrasattva and his consort, Dhatvishvari, or as Guru Padmasambhava and Yeshe Tsogyal.

See the mother as wisdom and the father as skillful means, empowering your consciousness through their union. In this way, conception is a great moment—an extraordinary opportunity to see everything as the mandala of the deities and a manifestation of transcendent wisdom. In full awareness of the innate purity of the world you are approaching, see the womb as a pureland, like Akanishtha.

Realized beings are conceived during a moment when both the mother and father are in a very beautiful state. One-pointedness, devotion, and inspiration have come together in such a powerful way that even the parents notice remarkable signs. Wonderful dreams and omens often accompany the conception and birth of a tulku, a reincarnated master or lama. Tulkus—reincarnated lamas—born this way are generally not totally enlightened. They have a good understanding of the true nature and are able to maintain a continuity of awareness throughout the process of transmigration. This allows them a degree of choice regarding their rebirth. When their fetus is completely developed, realized beings come forth with very special indications. For instance, they are often born without causing the mother any pain—her state may even be blissful and tranquil, accompanied by great signs like rainbows and other indications. Or perhaps immediately following the moment of birth the infant recites some mantra or says a few auspicious words. These babies take birth with great understanding and awareness. Many of them remember part of their life in the womb, and some even remember who they were before conception. A number of the great masters could remember everyone they'd ever been in the past quite clearly. These memories of past lives usually fade after the child is two or three years old, when they come under the influence of strong or newly acquired habit patterns.

Full Circle and the Importance of Practice

Following the bardo of becoming we're back again in the first bardo of birth and life. We've completed a big circle, sightseeing all around, and finally we're back where we started.

To really understand the bardos, it's necessary to practice. This is essential. Practice means to mingle our minds with what is positive—activities based on love and compassion, and the wisdom that arises through profound meditation on the true nature. One of the most valuable activities in our lives is spiritual practice. Although you may have many other priorities, try to understand why this effort is so important. Right now you can cultivate positive qualities and abilities that will reap untold benefits not only during this life, but also in endless future lives.

From the viewpoint of enlightened beings, transmigrators in the bardos seem as if they are caught in their own imaginary visions, like a child who encloses him or herself within a sandcastle and then makes a big fuss about getting out. To good practitioners, bardo phenomena are like magical projections—it's obvious they have no objective existence. The whole mirage completely evaporates into the luminosity of the true nature. That is why good practitioners no longer experience confusion and struggle.

For those who have already become enlightened by practicing in this or previous lifetimes, there are no bardo experiences at all. Everything is spontaneously transformed into the expanse of primordial wisdom. This is the state that was realized by Garab Dorje, Guru Padmasambhava, Vimalamitra, and other great masters. For them the bardo cycle is completely terminated, and there is no return to delusion.

Again, it's very useful to investigate how your current perception of things is any different from the visions you experience in the bardo of dreaming or the bardo of death. All phenomena, all perceptions, and all experiences encountered in any realm or bardo have the same nature. The experience we're having this very moment is essentially no different from any form of experience anywhere. Even though we may think this is solid and real, what we are seeing now is no more substantial than these other dimensions that we think are either less real or completely imaginary. In fact, they're all very much the same. There is no difference at all in their nature. We only think this experience is more real due to the strength of our habitual clinging. Presently, our body and environment seem to be solidly established and we're accustomed to grasping them, so we assume that these perceptions are real. Such concepts originate in our mind, which is immersed in duality and ego-clinging. In ignorance, the mind creates elaborate notions and fabrications, defines boundaries, builds walls, and invents rules and regulations that perpetuate conditions that are then suffered by that same mind. Ultimately, neither conventional "reality" nor the other bardo experiences exist in the way that we think they do. Our vision is obscured by duality, and the truth transcends conception.

The dualistic mind may not believe that the bardos exist in any sense, but this is a very narrow view. The bardos exist, but just in ways other than how we normally perceive things. They arise in the sphere of primordial wisdom, beyond subject-object dualism and all ego-clinging. They don't exist at all within the territory of dualistic concepts. For this reason, Buddha Shakyamuni taught that sentient beings live in a state of untruth—we arise in ignorance, and by relying on confusion and bewildered states, we create more confusion. Within this chaos we're so totally involved with delusion and suffering that we don't see that everything we experience is the result of what we ourselves have set in motion. Trouble returns to us like an echo. This is karma, and it must be understood.

Basically, there are two ways to purify karma: the tough way is through experience, and the smooth way is to purify it through practice. Meditate deeply on all of this, and then practice diligently to remove any obstacles to clear understanding.

Great beauty exists in the primordial expanse of the true nature, where all beings and worlds abide in perfect balance, beyond the limitations of dualistic thinking. Ego-clinging and attachment create obstacles and block our awareness of this. To overcome these temporary barriers, we practice and meditate according to the Buddha's teachings. We must learn to go beyond everything. That is what Avalokiteshvara meant in the Heart Sutra when he said "no eye, no ear, no nose, no tongue, no body, no mind." We have to break every possible style of ego-clinging and dualistic thinking. This is the goal of practice. The true nature will not be discovered outside of your mind. You will not encounter it by searching across the continents. The reality that transcends dualistic conceptions is directly revealed as the ground of mind. Discover this and abide in the truth of pristine awareness.

Realization depends on practice and meditation. Begin by generating bodhichitta and then visualize the Buddha or Guru Padmasambhava while reciting the Vajra Guru mantra. Receive the blessing energy from Guru Padmasambhava in the form of light, and mingle it inseparably with your mind. Meditate in that state without making any particular judgment or forming conceptions. This is the simplest way to meditate. Don't think practice has to be difficult or fancy. There's no need to take up an elaborate discipline.

There was a famous Indian master named Padampa Sangye, who came to Tibet around the eleventh century. He believed that practice didn't have to be very formal or complicated. As he explained it, the essence of practice is keeping the mind in its true nature, being more loving and compassionate, and maintaining this disposition. You don't have to go anywhere to get this because you already have this capacity within you. This is very true. You don't have to do anything difficult or

Padampa Sangye
Padma Samye Ling gonpa murals

make a big deal about practice. It's just something that you can do very simply in this or any moment. If you understand this, it becomes natural to develop courage and strength. The great nineteenth-century master Patrul Rinpoche said that wherever you go, you have your body, your speech, and your mind. Simply apply yourself to every situation with the bodhichitta motivation. You don't need any other ingredients. The spot where you're sitting now is as good as any. Actually, if you are loving and compassionate, you're already displaying the living form of the practice. Relax and radiate peace to all beings. In this way you may even consider yourself the vehicle of practice. That is what we should do.

Through practice we can accept and understand that death is a natural part of life. After birth and infancy we become children, teenagers, and grown-ups. Finally, we grow old and die. Knowing this, why are we so afraid and attached? It makes more sense to see every aspect of our life as part of a beautiful rainbow that has many different colors. By clearly knowing the truth, death becomes a once-in-a-lifetime opportunity to attain enlightenment.

Guru Padmasambhava summarizes the preciousness of this opportunity:

> *Never thinking death will come, we make long-term plans,*
> *Busy doing useless worldly tasks.*
> *If we return empty-handed our wishes will be wasted.*
> *We should know that the supreme Dharma is what we*
> *really need. Why don't we practice the supreme Dharma*
> *this very moment?*
> *It was said by the gracious lama himself,*
> *If you don't keep the lama's instructions safely in your mind,*
> *Won't you be deceiving yourself?*

Appendices

Questions and Answers on the Six Bardos

The following questions were answered by the Venerable Khenpo Rinpoches in the early 2000s during multiple discussions at the Padmasambhava Buddhist Center in West Palm Beach, Florida.

QUESTION: Is the process of the bardos and rebirth the same for all human beings regardless of whether they have Vajrayana training?

ANSWER: Yes, everybody goes through this process, whether or not they're a Buddhist. All sentient beings take birth. They all have five aggregates. They must have parents to contribute the two elements, and these elements are going to dissolve at death. Whether Buddhist or non-Buddhist, earth dissolves into water, water evaporates into fire, and all physical systems degenerate. The details of the visionary sequences may vary according to one's beliefs, but basically everybody will have similar experiences. According to the Vajrayana teachings, the bardo visions are reflections of your mental state, so the forms and images do not always have to appear in the same way for everybody. There may be differences in the color and the shape of the visions, but the main thing is to recognize them as

140

projections of your own mind. Therefore, in The Tibetan Book of the Dead, Guru Padmasambhava repeats, "Do not be afraid of your own visions. Do not be afraid when the wrathful deities appear. Do not be distracted. Recognize them as the display of your own mind." He repeats this again and again throughout these teachings. This is the basic message, the main point.

QUESTION: Eastern teachers postulate many births and deaths. Western teachers usually talk about only one birth and death. Are Western teachings incomplete?

ANSWER: In our hearts we feel that we're all considering the same thing and are just using different methods or maps. Western masters use a one-life model, and Eastern masters prefer a model that assumes many lives. One focuses exclusively on today, and the other provides a schedule for tomorrow and the day after tomorrow. There's only one true nature, and it doesn't have any divisions such as East or West. However, we strongly believe that everyone has to come to this fundamental recognition in order to be liberated. Simply believing in something could lead you to some kind of a higher state for a time, but then you might have to repeat the whole process again. On the other hand, if you come to understand the visions as projections of your own mind, you can really bring an end to this cycle. The forms of the visions are not as important as the recognition that what you see is part of your mind, without making dualistic judgments. To have hope and fear will not help us. If you have a good understanding and practice pure perception, you will realize that demons, gods, and everything abide in the single state of the true nature. Developing this understanding to the point of equanimity is the essential realization.

QUESTION: Do you think it's possible for human consciousness to be reborn in the animal realm or in the body of an insect or in one of the other realms?

ANSWER: Yes, definitely. We didn't mention this because we didn't want to scare you! With the appropriate causes and conditions, you could be reborn anywhere. There is a wide selection of openings.

QUESTION: If your consciousness is coming into the bardo of karmic possibilities and you've not practiced enough to have control over your rebirth, is your consciousness yanked out of the bardo all of a sudden and you find yourself in a womb?

ANSWER: You're not forcefully yanked, but your visions lead you there. You're drawn to a place that seems safe and comfortable. It happens naturally, in the same way that we like to go to the park. You see that environment and want to go there and rest. Since you're very unstable and moved about by karma, the womb looks like an attractive place to rest and find shelter, and once you're there you want to stay. There is no force indirectly causing this to happen other than your own karma. Once you are conceived in a womb, your active consciousness subsides and your awareness becomes very dark and dull. After you strongly identify with the developing fetus, your four skandhas* of feeling, perception, mental formation, and consciousness that were so restless during the previous bardos now exist in a more subtle, latent state.

QUESTION: For a great bodhisattva, is there a conscious decision to abide in a pure realm or to return and take rebirth?

ANSWER: It happens spontaneously. There isn't a moment of decision outside of one's bodhichitta commitment to serve sentient beings more effectively. When you merge with the true nature, you are completely aware. You know what you're doing and will do it in the clear light of wisdom. This is definitely a wonderful reward. From there it's perfectly natural to emanate in some form to help sentient beings. You'll manifest in whatever form is the most suitable, naturally feeling into the appropriate circumstance and following that

---

*The skandhas are the psycho-spiritual elements that comprise a person's existence. There are five: in this case, matter, in the form of the four elements of earth, air, fire, and water coming together as an aggregate form, has not yet manifest. The other four skandhas that arise at this time are physical sensations or feelings, perceptions, mental formations, and awareness or consciousness. It is said that by meditating on the skandhas, one can overcome self-grasping, the tendency to think that the self is unique, independent, and permanent.

course. The power of compassion spontaneously orients the emanation without any effort. You could enjoy the dharmakaya state for a while before manifesting in sambhogakaya and nirmanakaya forms in response to the needs of sentient beings, but you're not limited to human birth. You can manifest as a god, an animal, or whatever would be most beneficial.

QUESTION: What happens if you don't choose a womb? Would you not take birth at all?

ANSWER: Generally, you can't make that choice. There is nothing causing you to stay there. Your karmic winds will carry you, and you won't be able to turn away, so you must choose. This is an opportunity.

QUESTION: If a person commits suicide, is there karmic retribution in the bardo? Do they have to stay longer? What happens in the bardo after suicide?

ANSWER: Generally, everybody follows the same pattern of dissolution. But if someone dies while they're angry and holding very strong attachments such as jealousy, this could extend their stay in the bardo. Due to deep attachment and clinging to negative emotions, they might continue to hover in the bardo, but it won't necessarily always happen this way. A lot depends on their last moment of consciousness before death. If they aren't particularly angry or jealous, then their disposition could change, and they would have a normal bardo experience. But to die under the influence of powerful emotions could completely change this situation.

QUESTION: I had an experience after a family member died in which I felt like they were present with me and trying to help me by telling me something. Does this mean that they were still in the bardo and trying to communicate due to attachment?

ANSWER: I don't think so. Sometimes that happens, but if you experience warm feelings and a sense of goodness, this is usually a nice reverberation they have left behind. In Tibet we call this *lha* (or *bla*), which is the powerful personal energy that holds something intact. For example, even though a person may have died a long time ago, there may still be blessing potential that remains from their being a good person with strong altruistic motivations. This lha is not physical or mental—it's the power resonance of that person and may remain for a long time. A good person has good energy and a bad person has bad energy. They say that an especially good person's energy can affect family members for quite a few generations.

QUESTION: Is the world a chain of existence and nonexistence happening very rapidly in succession along a timeline, or is it all within an eternal moment?

ANSWER: The world is based on continual change. Everything is transformed one instant after another. This doesn't only apply to the external world—even what you call your "self" changes from moment to moment. These subtle instants are discrete, independent states that occur very rapidly, one following another, continuously. The first moment is not the second moment, and the second moment is not the third moment. These "sparks" are also directly dependent on one another. The first becomes the cause of the second, and the second becomes the cause of the third. Everything consists of these chains of moving moments. In Buddhism this is called "relative truth." We're all experiencing momentary change on the relative level. But on the absolute level things neither exist nor do they not exist. The categories of existence and nonexistence are part of a conceptual game. The absolute level is beyond existence and nonexistence.

QUESTION: I've read that there are mind tulkus, speech tulkus, and body tulkus that all emanate from the same being. Do these three ever incarnate at the same time?

ANSWER: Why not? That is their choice. They can all manifest at once or keep some time between them. They don't have to follow any laws. They can do whatever they like.

QUESTION: Concerning the four kinds of enlightened deaths, you said that practitioners give up doubts and fears, but do they really give up hope, too?

ANSWER: Yes, they also give up hope. They have no hope or fear; they go beyond both of these. Hope and fear go together. In fact, they're very good friends. If you lose one, then the other is kind of disappointed and leaves, too.

QUESTION: How did you figure all this out?

ANSWER: We have to refer to Buddha Shakyamuni and Guru Padmasambhava. These are their teachings. Guru Padmasambhava compassionately condensed them so that they could be presented in a simple form. In Buddhism we believe that when you discover primordial wisdom and stabilize this realization, you become fully aware so that there is nothing impeding your knowledge of all things. You can understand everything in detail, even very subtle phenomena. Primordial wisdom is that powerful. Guru Padmasambhava and the Buddha perfectly realized the primordial nature, and since their wisdom is actively involved in the liberation of all sentient beings, in the spirit of compassion and loving-kindness they have given these teachings for our benefit.

QUESTION: No one ever came back and explained what happens after death?

ANSWER: In Tibet there have been some people who have returned from death. Their outer breath stops completely so that they are effectively dead, but their inner winds are somehow suspended. They might remain like this for an entire week and then come back and explain what they have been through. Generally in Tibet they don't cremate the body immediately after death. They keep it around for at least three days, and many times people will wait forty-nine days, so there's a lot of time to come back! Those who come back are known as *delogs*. Often they become very passionate spiritual teachers. There were six or seven renowned delogs, particularly in eastern Tibet. One woman, Kadema, who died and came back, related the details of her experience in a book. It may have been destroyed by the Chinese government, but it was all written down at one point. She met many bardo beings who gave her messages to deliver to people she didn't even know, who lived in different parts of the country. The bardo beings gave their family names to her, described the places where they lived, and asked her to deliver messages. When she returned to life she delivered them to the right people. Many of the visions and experiences of the woman corresponded exactly to the descriptions given in bardo teachings.

QUESTION: You were talking about how everyone perceives things differently. I was wondering if enlightened people perceive things similarly?

ANSWER: Definitely, but even among the buddhas we can see some individual differences in the ways they express their wisdom. More specifically, in Buddhism there are two kinds of wisdom: wisdom that knows all phenomena, and wisdom that knows the true nature of all phenomena. Buddhas can see the world we see, but they also see it as it is. Ultimately, a buddha's vision cannot be explained. The famous Indian master Dharmakirti wrote that the realization of an enlightened being is inconceivable.

QUESTION: What happens if you rarely dream?

ANSWER: You are in a state known as "deep sleep." The five consciousnesses have entered the sixth consciousness of dualistic mind, and the sixth consciousness is submerged in the alaya. The experience of this is deep, dreamless sleep. Practice and meditation will help lighten the mind and activate dreams.

QUESTION: In our society, if someone is really sick and dying in the hospital, instead of letting the process happen naturally they're either given chemicals or are attached to machines. What does this do to their bardo journey? How does it affect the process?

ANSWER: According to the bardo teachings, it's important to let people die naturally and not interfere with futile techniques or drugs that dull awareness. If it's not going to cure them, perhaps it would be better not to employ such means. We've heard about these machines; some people are left on them for a long time, and it doesn't seem like it's really helping them. If their time has expired and we don't allow them to depart, we're holding them back and trying to hang on in the wrong way. We should definitely use medicines and different techniques as long as they are useful. But when it's time to leave, it's better to just let it happen.

QUESTION: Can your progress be hindered if you are connected to machines?

ANSWER: That depends. If you're a very good practitioner we really don't think anything will hinder you. But if you're just a beginning practitioner it could definitely interfere with your progress and create a big distraction. At the time of death the inner sensations and feelings caused by the machine may be very strong and affect your ability to concentrate. If your mind is not very clear at that point you could remain in a dull state for a long time.

QUESTION: Is the mental body of a bardo being the same as a ghost?

ANSWER: Ghosts are called *yidaks* in Tibetan and *pretas* in Sanskrit. They belong to the hungry ghost realm. These beings have already gone through the bardo and have taken rebirth as hungry ghosts. Birth as a hungry ghost is due to prolonged greed and attachment. Beings transmigrating in the bardo are not ghosts and do not see ghosts. Ghosts exist in another realm. Beings in the same state can see one another. Transmigrators only see those who are also in transmigration. They can't perceive other levels of existence. This is why we don't see any invisible beings, we only see one another. The Buddha assured us that there are definitely a multitude of invisible beings everywhere. Although we rarely interact with one another, invisible beings can easily see us because humans are resplendent with the qualities of buddha nature. Our capacity for love and compassion makes us more powerful than most invisible beings. Therefore, when you're doing a ritual, ask the invisible beings to come, even if they don't want to. The Buddha's message is one of peace and harmony, and we need to get along with everyone. To insure that we're not trespassing and to demonstrate that we are truly harmless, we acknowledge our intention to realize our buddha nature for the benefit of all other beings, visible and invisible. So at the beginning of any Vajrayana ceremony it's good to ask for the approval of the local invisible beings. This is the meaning behind the white and red torma offerings that precede most Nyingma sadhanas. These practices are designed to make friends with the invisible beings of the local area.

QUESTION: Is there a world soul, and if so are there bardo places and reincarnations for the cosmos?

ANSWER: In Buddhism there is no belief in a universal consciousness. Without closely observing and investigating we can emotionally evoke the notion of a universal mind, like a big dome that covers everything. But if we examine this very carefully through study and deep contemplation we will find that there is no universal consciousness.

QUESTION: You mentioned that there are different approaches to enlightenment, citing Garab Dorje as an example of the first kind, while Padmasambhava illustrated the second kind. What is the difference between these two types?

ANSWER: Garab Dorje is an example of the type of person who realizes enlightenment instantly. Guru Padmasambhava embodied the second way in that he received teachings and afterward became realized. Garab Dorje immediately recognized it without hesitating, whereas for Guru Padmasambhava and Vimalamitra, a few moments passed before they understood perfectly. This is why we study under Guru Padmasambhava, because in our own case there is a temporal gap between receiving the teachings and attainment. There's also a third category of practitioners who usually take longer than a few moments but still manage to achieve realization within their lifetime. In terms of their enlightenment they're all identical, but the way they approach realization is slightly different. All of these great masters are considered extraordinary practitioners because they became enlightened within one lifetime and attained the rainbow body. This is not a method, but a spontaneous process in which the physical body is completely transformed into light. At the time of physical death these realized beings melted or dissolved their body into light, leaving no trace. They just became pure light.

Dedication of Merit

May the victory banner of the fearless teachings of the
  ancient tradition be raised.
May the victorious drum of the teaching and practice of
  Dharma resound in the ten directions.
May the lion's roar of reasoning pervade the three
  places.
May the light of unequaled virtues increase.*

Dharmapalas who made commitments to the lamas of the
  three lineages,
Dharmapalas of the three groups, summon up your superior
  mighty powers.
Help quickly disseminate throughout the three worlds,
The treasure of the pure Dharma lineages of the three
  enlightened beings.†

---

*These first four lines come from "Aspiration Prayer" by Jamgon Mipham Rinpoche.

†Dharmapalas refer to numerous great Dharma protectors, benevolent enlightened and unenlightened beings who appear ferociously so as to instill terror in negative spirits and those who seek to destroy the Dharma. On a more inner level, Dharma protectors also refer to whatever protects the mind from losing recognition of its innate wisdom and compassion, or rigpa. Source for these four lines unknown.

May all the temples and monasteries,
All the readings and recitations of the Dharma flourish.
May the sangha always be in harmony,
And may their aspirations be achieved.*

At this very moment, for the peoples and nations of the earth,
May not even the names disease, famine, war, and suffering
be heard.
But rather may pure conduct, merit, wealth, and prosperity
increase,
And may supreme good fortune and well-being always arise.†

---

*These four lines come from Shantideva.

†These last four lines were spoken by H. H. Dudjom Rinpoche Jigdral Yeshe Dorje.

Meditation on Absolute Wisdom

The Moment of Death Sutra

The Moment of Death Sutra is a profound teaching by Buddha Shakyamuni that can be recited anytime to inspire our Dharma practice and rekindle our understanding of relative impermanence as well as the unchanging, absolute true nature of mind. Recite this in whatever language is helpful for you to connect to the meaning. As we approach death, this might be particularly helpful to remind us of our insubstantial awakened awareness, which is the deathless nature of mind.

ༀ། །འདའ་ཀ་ཡེ་ཤེས་ངེས་དོན་བསྒོམ་པའི་མདོ་བཞུགས་སོ།

DA KA YE SHE NGE DÖN GOM PE DHO ZHUK SO
Meditation on Absolute Wisdom:
The Moment of Death Sutra

རྒྱ་གར་སྐད་དུ། ཨཱརྱ་ཨ་ཏ་ཇྙ་ན་ནཱ་མ་མ་ཧཱ་ཡཱ་ན་སཱུ་ཏྲ།

JA GAR KE DU   **ARYA ATA JNANA NAMA MAHAYANA SUTRA**
In Sanskrit: Arya Ata Jnana Nama Mahayana Sutra

བོད་སྐད་དུ། འཕགས་པ་འདའ་ཀ་ཡེ་ཤེས་ཞེས་བྱ་བ་ཐེག་པ་
ཆེན་པོའི་མདོ།

PÖ KE DU   **PAKPA DAKA YESHE ZHE JAWA TEGPA**
                 CHENPÖ DHO
In Tibetan: Pakpa Daka Yeshe Zhe Jawa Tegpa
                 Chenpö Dho

(In English: The Mahayana Sutra Known as the
                 Noble Wisdom of the Moment of Death)

སངས་རྒྱས་དང་བྱང་ཆུབ་སེམས་དཔའ་ཐམས་ཅད་ལ་ཕྱག་འཚལ་ལོ།

SANG JE DANG JANG CHUP SEM PA TAM CHE LA CHAK TSAL LO
Homage to all buddhas and bodhisattvas!

འདི་སྐད་བདག་གིས་ཐོས་པ་དུས་གཅིག་ན།

DI KE DAK GI TÖ PA DÜ CHIK NA
Thus I have heard.

བཅོམ་ལྡན་འདས་འོག་མིན་རྒྱལ་པོའི་ཁང་བཟང་ལ་བཞུགས་ཏེ།

CHOM DEN DE OG MIN JAL PÖ KHANG ZANG LA ZHUK TE
When the Blessed One was dwelling in the palace of the King of Ogmin,

འཁོར་ཐམས་ཅད་ལ་ཆོས་སྟོན་པ་དང་།

KHOR TAM CHE LA CHÖ TÖN PA DANG
Teaching the Dharma to all beings around him,

བྱང་ཆུབ་སེམས་དཔའ་ནམ་མཁའི་སྙིང་པོས་བཅོམ་ལྡན་འདས་ལ་

ཕྱག་འཚལ་ནས།

JANG CHUP SEM PA NAM KHE NYING PÖ CHOM DEN DE LA CHAK TSAL NE
The bodhisattva Akashagarbha prostrated to the Blessed One,

འདི་སྐད་ཅེས་གསོལ་ཏོ།

DI KE CHE SOL TO
And thus respectfully said,

བཅོམ་ལྡན་འདས་བྱང་ཆུབ་སེམས་དཔའ་ནམ་འཆི་ཀ་མའི་སེམས་ཇི་

ལྟར་བལྟ་བར་བགྱི།

CHOM DEN DE JANG CHUP SEM PA NAM CHI KA ME SEM JI TAR TA WAR JI
"Blessed One, when a bodhisattva is dying, how should he focus his mind?"

དེ་ནས་བཅོམ་ལྡན་འདས་ཀྱི་བཀའ་སྩལ་པ།

TE NE CHOM DEN DE CHI KA TSAL PA
Then the Blessed One replied:

ནམ་མཁའི་སྙིང་པོ་བྱང་ཆུབ་སེམས་དཔའ་ནམ་འཆི་བའི་ཚེ།

NAM KHE NYING PO JANG CHUP SEM PA NAM CHI WE TSE
"Akashagarbha, when the time comes for a bodhisattva to die,

འདའ་ཀའ་ཡེ་ཤེས་བསྒོམ་པར་བྱའོ།

DA KA YE SHE GÖM PAR CHA O
He should meditate on the wisdom of the moment of death.

དེ་ལ་འདའ་ཀའ་ཡེ་ཤེས་ནི།

TE LA DA KA YE SHE NI
Such is the wisdom of the moment of death:

ཆོས་ཐམས་ཅད་རང་བཞིན་གྱིས་རྣམ་པར་དག་པས་ན།

CHÖ TAM CHE RANG ZHIN JI NAM PAR DAK PE NA
All phenomena by nature are completely pure;

དངོས་པོ་མེད་པའི་འདུ་ཤེས་རབ་ཏུ་བསྒོམ་པར་བྱའོ།

NGÖ PO ME PE DU SHE RAB TU GÖM PAR CHA O
Therefore, meditate with the understanding of insubstantiality.

ཆོས་ཐམས་ཅད་བྱང་ཆུབ་ཀྱི་སེམས་སུ་འདུས་པས་ན།

CHÖ TAM CHE JANG CHUP CHI SEM SU DÜ PE NA
All phenomena are embodied by awakened awareness;

སྙིང་རྗེ་ཆེན་པོའི་འདུ་ཤེས་རབ་ཏུ་བསྒོམ་པར་བྱའོ།

NYING JE CHEN PÖ DU SHE RAB TU GÖM PAR CHA O
Therefore, meditate with great compassion.

ཆོས་ཐམས་ཅད་རང་བཞིན་གྱིས་མི་དམིགས་ཤིང་འོད་གསལ་བས་ན།

CHÖ TAM CHE RANG ZHIN JI MI MIK SHING Ö SAL WE NA
The nature of all phenomena is clear light beyond conception;

དངོས་པོ་ཅི་ལ་ཡང་མི་ཆགས་པའི་འདུ་ཤེས་རབ་ཏུ་བསྒོམ་པར་བྱའོ།

NGÖ PO CHI LA YANG MI CHAK PE DU SHE RAB TU GÖM PAR CHA O
Therefore, meditate with the understanding of non-attachment to any object.

སེམས་རྟོགས་ན་ཡེ་ཤེས་ཡིན་པས་ན།

SEM TOK NA YE SHE YIN PE NA
Realizing the nature of the mind is wisdom;

སངས་རྒྱས་གཞན་དུ་མི་བཙལ་བའི་འདུ་ཤེས་རབ་ཏུ་བསྒོམ་པར་བྱའོ།

SANG JE ZHEN DU MI TSAL WE DU SHE RAB TU GÖM PAR CHA O
Therefore, meditate with the understanding that there is no need to search for the Buddha elsewhere."

བཅོམ་ལྡན་འདས་ཀྱིས་ཚིགས་སུ་བཅད་དེ་བཀའ་སྩལ་པ།

CHOM DEN DE CHI TSIK SU CHE TE KA TSAL PA
Then the Blessed One gave this teaching in verse:

ཆོས་རྣམས་རང་བཞིན་རྣམ་དག་པས།

CHÖ NAM RANG ZHIN NAM DAK PE
"As all phenomena by nature are completely pure,

དངོས་པོ་མེད་པའི་འདུ་ཤེས་བསྒོམ།

NGÖ PO ME PE DU SHE GÖM
Meditate with the understanding of insubstantiality.

 བྱང་ཆུབ་སེམས་དང་རབ་ལྡན་པས།

JANG CHUP SEM DANG RAB DEN PE
As awakened awareness is the very nature of the mind,

སྙིང་རྗེ་ཆེན་པོའི་འདུ་ཤེས་བསྒོམ།

NYING JE CHEN PÖ DU SHE GÖM
Meditate with great compassion.

རང་བཞིན་མི་དམིགས་འོད་གསལ་བས།

RANG ZHIN MI MIK Ö SAL WE
As the nature of the mind is clear light beyond conception,

དངོས་པོ་ལ་འང་མི་ཆགས་བསྒོམ།

NGÖ PO LA ANG MI CHAK GÖM
Meditate on it without attachment to any object.

སེམས་ནི་ཡེ་ཤེས་འབྱུང་བའི་རྒྱུ།

SEM NI YE SHE JUNG WE JU
As wisdom arises from the mind itself,

སངས་རྒྱས་གཞན་དུ་མ་ཚོལ་ཅིག

SANG JE ZHEN DU MA TSOL CHIK
Do not search for the Buddha elsewhere."

བཅོམ་ལྡན་འདས་ཀྱིས་དེ་སྐད་ཅེས་བཀའ་སྩལ་པ་དང་།

CHOM DEN DE CHI TE KE CHE KA TSAL PA DANG
When the Blessed One spoke these words,

བྱང་ཆུབ་སེམས་དཔའ་ནམ་མཁའི་སྙིང་པོ་ལ་སོགས་པའི་འཁོར་ཐམས་

ཅད་རབ་ཏུ་དགའ་སྟེ།

JANG CHUP SEM PA NAM KHE NYING PO LA SOK PE KHOR TAM CHE RAB TU GA TE
The bodhisattva Akashagarbha and all the assemblies were filled with great joy,

བཅོམ་ལྡན་འདས་ཀྱིས་གསུངས་པ་ལ་མངོན་པར་བསྟོད་དོ།

CHOM DEN DE CHI SUNG PA LA NGÖN PAR TÖ DO
And praised what the Blessed One had said.

འཕགས་པ་འདའ་ཀ་ཡེ་ཤེས་ཞེས་བྱ་བ་ཐེག་པ་ཆེན་པོའི་མདོ་རྫོགས་སོ།།

This completes the Noble Wisdom of the Moment of Death, a Mahayana sutra.

This translation was completed by Venerable Khenpo Tsewang Dongyal Rinpoche and edited by Peter De Niro in 2011 at Padma Samye Ling.

Glossary

Abhidharma (Tib. *ngon pa*): The third of the "Three Baskets" (Skt. *Tripitaka*) of the Buddha's teachings, the other two being the vinaya and the sutras. The word *Abhidharma* is alternately translated into English as "directly cognizing" or "vividly seeing" (Skt. *abhi*) the teachings (Skt. *dharma*), or "about the teachings." This implies that a person directly sees the Dharma, without exaggeration or imagination. The Abhidharma includes teaching on Buddhist psychology and logic, descriptions of the universe, the steps on the path to enlightenment, descriptions of the different kinds of beings, and refutations of mistaken beliefs.

alaya (Tib. *kun gzhi*): The "all-ground" or "subconscious storehouse" is literally translated as "foundation of all things." It is the basis of mind and both pure and impure phenomena, and all karmic imprints are stored here. In some cases *alaya* is a synonym for *buddha nature* or *dharmakaya*, the recognition of which forms the basis of all pure phenomena. In other cases *alaya* refers to the neutral state of duality mind that has not been recognized as innate wakefulness. In this latter case, the alaya forms the basis for samsaric experience.

bardo (Tib. *bar do*): The Tibetan word *bardo* is often translated as "intermediate state." The Nyingma school describes six principal bardos: (1) the bardo of birth and life (Tib. *skye gnas bar do*), (2) the bardo of the dream state (Tib. *rmi lam bar do*), (3) the bardo of meditation (Tib. *bsam gtan bar do*), (4) the bardo of dying (Tib. *'chi kha'I bar do*), (5) the bardo of the luminosity of the true nature (Tib. *chos nyid bar do*), and (6) the bardo of becoming (Tib. *srid pa bar do*). See also **Zhitro**.

Bardo Thodrol: The terma teaching given by Guru Padmasambhava that includes extensive details on all of the bardos. Its title is translated into English as "Liberation through Hearing in the Bardo," although it is commonly known as The Tibetan Book of the Dead.

bhumi (Tib. *sa bcu*): There are many ways to describe the practices and stages of realization that progressively unfold as one engages in the Buddhist path. Among these, the ten bodhisattva levels or stages are particularly renowned. On the first bodhisattva level, great emptiness is seen as it is, and the entire universe is perceived as the magical display of the true nature, which brings forth utter satisfaction and great joy. The second through tenth stages achieve the deepest realization available through meditation, until one reaches the eleventh level when pristine buddha nature is fully actualized. At this stage, samsara and nirvana are equal, no more practice is needed, and great benefits can be accomplished for others. This is total enlightenment. The tenth stage is sometimes subdivided into three or six additional categories, for a total of thirteen or sixteen bhumis.

bodhichitta (Tib. *byang chub kyi sems*): Literally, the "mind of enlightenment," comprising impartial love, compassion, and wisdom for all beings. Relative bodhichitta indicates the wish to attain buddhahood for the sake of all parent sentient beings by practicing the path of love, compassion, and wisdom. This can be further divided into aspiring bodhichitta and actualizing bodhichitta. The former indicates the altruistic intention to usher all sentient beings into a permanent state of enlightenment by achieving liberation oneself, whereas the latter indicates actually engaging in bodhichitta activities. In contrast, *absolute bodhichitta* is a synonym for the nature of mind, the open, vast clarity of awareness itself. Absolute bodhichitta recognizes that all beings are primordially enlightened—there is no liberator, no deluded beings, and no act of liberation, since nothing ever moves from the absolute sphere of the dharmadhatu, or rigpa.

Abiding in this great immovable resting is the ultimate bodhichitta. It is always important to practice the union of relative and absolute bodhichitta. The Venerable Rinpoches often teach that if at first it is difficult to practice absolute bodhichitta, there is no need to worry—by practicing relative bodhichitta, the mind will gradually become more relaxed, peaceful, and open, eventually expanding into the ultimate state of absolute bodhichitta. See also **bodhisattva**, **dharmadatu**, and **rigpa**.

bodhisattva (Tib. *byang chub sems dpa'*): Literally, "courageous one for enlightenment," a bodhisattva is an advanced Mahayana practitioner who traverses the five paths and ten bodhisattva levels. Such a practitioner is so committed to working for the benefit and welfare of others that on one level he or she chooses to remain in samsara in order to bring all beings to full enlightenment. Practically speaking, however, the bodhisattva takes relative and absolute bodhichitta as the essence of their practice and strives to attain complete enlightenment, after which point they will be able to benefit beings much more effectively. See also **bhumi**, **bodhichitta**, and **Mahayana**.

buddha (Tib. *sangs rgyas*): The general term *buddha* denotes one who has completely awakened from the fundamental ignorance of the two obscurations (conflicting emotions and limiting cognitive habits) and developed unceasing pristine cognition of the buddha nature. Having cultivated every positive quality to their utmost limit, a buddha has traversed the bodhisattva levels and eliminated all obscurations to true knowledge. Thus he or she enjoys the five fruitional aspects of a buddha: enlightened (1) body, (2) speech, (3) mind, (4) qualities, and (5) activities, or the "five wheels of inexhaustible adornment" (Tib. *mi zad rgyan gyi 'khor lo lnga*). Buddha Shakyamuni was the fourth of one thousand buddhas who will appear during the current fortunate aeon. See also **Buddhadharma** and **buddha nature**.

Buddhadharma (Tib. *sangs rgyas kyi chos*): The Sanskrit word *dharma* has about ten different meanings, but here it refers specifically to the teachings of Buddha Shakyamuni. In general there are two aspects of the Buddhadharma: *transmission*, or teachings that are actually given; and the Dharma of *realization*, or the stages that are attained by applying the teachings. What distinguishes the Dharma as such is the presence of "four seals" or "four marks" (Tib. *bka' rtags kyi phyag rgya bzhi*) that separate worldly teachings from transcendent ones. These are often given as follows: (1) all compounded things are impermanent; (2) all afflictive emotions are of the nature of suffering; (3) all phenomena are empty and devoid of a self-identity; and (4) nirvana is peace (or nirvana is beyond extremes). See also **buddha** and **buddha nature**.

buddha nature (Skt. *Tathagatagarbha*; Tib. *de bzhin gshegs pa'i snying po*): Buddha nature is the inherent richness nature of all sentient beings. An essential teaching of both the Mahayana sutras and the tantras, it is known by many names, including "absolute bodhichitta," "Prajnaparamita," "Mother of All the Buddhas," "Madhyamaka," and "Mahamudra," among others. In the context of the inner tantras and Dzogchen in particular, buddha nature is often called "the inseparable union of primordially pure and spontaneously inherent qualities" of mind, recognized through the Dzogchen practices of trekcho and togal. See also **buddha**, **Buddhadharma**, **tathagatagarbha**, **togal**, and **trekcho**.

completion stage (Tib. *rdzogs rim*): One of the two stages of Vajrayana practice, the other being the creation (or generation) stage. The completion stage focuses primarily on the vajra mind through one of two techniques: (1) the completion stage with characteristics, and (2) the completion stage without characteristics. Examples of the first include dream yoga, phowa, and other practices, also known as "skillful means practices." By visualizing and meditating on the actual, inherent qualities within our body, including our channels, winds, and essence elements, we discover great bliss-emptiness, the absolute Guru Padmasambhava. In all these practices we hold, visualize, and concentrate on something. In the completion stage without characteristics, we don't concentrate on anything but simply rest in the fresh, present state and behold the panoramic view of outer and inner phenomena without any boundaries. Examples of this include the Dzogchen practices of **trekcho** and **togal**. See also **creation stage**, **togal**, **trekcho**, and **Vajrayana**.

creation stage (Tib. *bskyed rim*): One of the two stages of Vajrayana practice, the other being the completion stage. The creation (or generation) stage is related to Mahayoga, in which everything is seen as the indestructible body, speech, and mind of enlightenment, or the "three vajra states." Creation-stage practice can generally be divided into visualization and mantra recitation. After we establish the visualization of the deities, we recite their mantra. When during Vajrayana practice we visualize our environment and ourselves as enlightened, we are bringing out our inner, self-born awareness wisdom without being disturbed by duality and habitual patterns. We're discovering the splendid qualities of our inner primordial wisdom, which then shines out through our body and speech. Our body becomes primordial wisdom form, and our speech becomes primordial wisdom sound. When the sunlight of our inborn nature of primordial wisdom shines through our speech and body, we're inseparable from Guru Padmasambhava. In fact, we *are* Guru Padmasambhava. Our nature of self-born wisdom awareness is absolute Guru Padmasambhava. See also **completion stage** and **Vajrayana**.

dakini (Tib. *mkha' 'gro ma*): The Tibetan term for dakini, *khandro*, literally means "space voyager" or "sky voyager," referring to a female being who has recognized the empty nature of all phenomena. Dakinis are feminine spiritual beings who engage in enlightened activities and have attained either mundane or supramundane spiritual accomplishments; they are also female tantric deities who serve and protect the Buddhist doctrine and practitioners. Dakinis have always played an important role in guarding and transmitting the Vajrayana teachings. One of the Three Roots, they confer buddha activities on a practitioner, in contrast with the Vajra Guru (Tib. *rdo rje slob dpon*), who bestows blessings, and the yidam (Tib. *yi dam*), who bestows accomplishments. This term can also refer to an enlightened female practitioner of the Vajrayana. The male counterpart of the dakini is the *daka*. See **Three Roots** and **yidam**.

deity: Rather than referring to God or gods, in Buddhism a deity (or deities) is a synonym for an enlightened being or buddha who fully realizes the empty, interdependent nature of everything. In meditation, practitioners visualize certain deities that reflect the different aspects of the buddha nature in order to connect more completely with their own buddha nature, as well as to connect with the enlightened nature of all forms.

dependent origination (Skt. *pratityasamutpada*; Tib. *tendrel du jungwa*): Everything is interdependent and connected to everything else. This is not only true for objects and entities in the physical world, but for mental states as well. It might appear as if individual phenomena are distinct and separate, but the truth is that nothing has an independent existence or can do or be anything on its own. This disparity between appearance and reality is what great masters mean when they say "Everything is an illusion." Through interdependence we know emptiness. It is emptiness that allows things to interact and develop, to change and grow. Without emptiness, which is sometimes likened to space, there's no possibility and no room for any activity. Because of this Nagarjuna said, "Since everything is a part of the interdependent coordination system, everything is emptiness." See **emptiness**.

devotion (Skt. *bhakthi*; Tib. *dad pa*): Devotion is the root of all accomplishment, and the practice of Vajrayana is impossible without it. The three stages of devotion are: (1) initial, interested devotion (Tib. *dang ba'i dad pa*); (2) devotion of intense longing (Tib. *'dod pa'i dad pa*); and (3) final devotion of unshakable certainty (Tib. *phyir mi ldog pa'i dad pa*). A variation of these three types of devotion or faith is described by Longchenpa: lucid faith, desirous faith, and the faith of conviction. The first entails a lucid frame of mind that arises in reference to the Three Jewels. The second concerns the desire to take up the Three Jewels very closely in the heart and develop a clear sense of the four renunciation thoughts. And the third involves having conviction in the principle of karmic causality. See **Three Jewels**.

Dharma (Tib. *Chos*). See **Buddhadharma**.

dharmakaya (Tib. *chos sku*): The dharmakaya is the ultimate nature and essence of enlightened mind on the absolute level. On the relative level it indicates the primordial purity of phenomena related to the fact that all phenomena are equal in a state of great emptiness. The dharmakaya is uncreated, free from conceptual elaboration, naturally radiant, empty of inherent existence, and spacious like the sky. Although by its very nature it cannot adequately be expressed in words, the dharmakaya is the very suchness (Skt. *tathatha*) that pervades all phenomena—all subjects, objects, and actions. See also **emptiness**, **nirmanakaya**, and **sambhogakaya**.

dharmadhatu (Tib. *chos kyi dbyings*): Literally, "the realm of phenomena." Dharmadhatu refers to the suchness in which emptiness and dependently-arisen appearances are inseparable. This is the nature of mind and phenomena—emptiness—that is free from arising, dwelling, and ceasing.

dharmapala (Tib. *chos skyong*): Either a wisdom or worldly deity who serves as a guardian of the Buddhist teachings. As stated in the *Rangjung Yeshe Tibetan-English Dictionary of Buddhist Culture*, "They are sometimes emanations of buddhas or bodhisattvas, and sometimes spirits and demons who have been subjugated and bound under oath by great practitioners such as Guru Padmasambhava. Among the best known are Ekajati, Mahakala, Dza Rahula, and Damchen Dorje Lekpa."

dharmata (Tib. *chonyi*): Suchness, the true nature of reality, the absolute nature, or intrinsic reality.

Dhyani Buddhas (Tib. *ton pa nga*): The five buddhas that preside over the five buddha families of Vajra, Ratna, Padma, Karma, and Buddha, which represent five aspects of the innate qualities of our enlightened essence. The Dhyani Buddhas of the center are Vairochana and Mamaki, whose color is usually blue and represent the Buddha family. The Dhyani Buddhas of the east are Vajrasattva-Akshobhya and Dhatvishvari, who are white and represent the Vajra family. The Dhyani Buddhas of the south are Ratnasambhava and Lochana, who are yellow and represent the Ratna family. The Dhyani Buddhas of the west are Amitabha and Pandaravasini, who are red and represent the Padma family. The Dhyani Buddhas of the north are Amoghasiddhi and Tara, who are green and represent the Karma family.

Dzogchen (Skt. *Mahasandhi*; Tib. *rdzogs chen*): Often translated as "Great Perfection" or "Great Completion," Dzogchen represents the highest teachings of Buddha Shakyamuni, comprising the ninth and last *yana* of the Nyingma school. The term *Great Perfection* can be understood to mean that all the Buddha's teachings are utterly complete and perfected in Dzogchen; thus all nine yanas are encompassed, without contradiction, in this, the pinnacle of every vehicle. The Dzogchen teachings were first brought to Tibet in the eighth century CE and taught by three principal masters: Guru Padmasambhava, Panchen Vimalamitra, and Vairochana. These teachings can be subdivided into three principal lineages: the Mind Class (Tib. *sems sde*), the Space Class (Tib. *klong sde*), and the Pith Instruction Class (Tib. *man ngag gi sde*). Through the practice of Dzogchen, all enlightened attributes are effortlessly perfected in one's own intrinsic, primordial awareness, known as *rigpa*. According to the Dzogchen teachings, the nature of awareness is empty in essence (dharmakaya), luminous in nature (sambhogakaya), and unconfined in capacity (nirmanakaya). See also **dharmakaya, nirmanakaya, Nyingma, rigpa, sambhogakaya,** and **yana.**

guru (Tib. *bla ma*): Among the Three Roots of Vajrayana practice, the guru is the source of blessings. It is often said that one's guru is even kinder than the Buddha, since he or she directly bestows the empowerments, transmissions, and lineage instructions that lead to enlightenment. Guru Yoga is a profound technique in which a practitioner merges his or her mind with the wisdom mind of the guru. See also **Three Roots.**

emptiness (Skt. *sunyata*; Tib. *tong pa nyi*): The ultimate nature of mind and all external phenomena, which both lack an inherent existence that is singular, independent, and permanent. In other words, everything is "empty" of fixed qualities, and therefore is entirely interdependent and relational in nature.

Four Boundless Qualities (Skt. *Catvaryapramanani*; Tib. *Tshad Med Bzhi*): Also called the Four Immeasurables, this is the essence of aspirational bodhichitta, which includes infinite love (Tib. *byams pa*), infinite compassion (Tib. *snying rje*), infinite sympathetic joy (Tib. *Dga' ba*), and infinite equanimity (Tib. *btang snyoms*) for all beings without exception. See also **bodhichitta**.

Guhyagarbha Tantra (Skt. *Guhyagarbha Mayajala*; Tib. *Gsang Ba'i Snying Po*): In English, "The Secret Essence Tantra: The Net of Magical Illusions" is the "King of All Tantras." It is a root tantra of the Mayayoga vehicle of the inner tantras, which is specifically related to the mandalas of enlightened body, speech, mind, quality, and activity. See **Mahayoga**.

Hinayana (Tib. *theg pa dman pa*): Literally "Lesser Vehicle," this group of Buddhist teachings is so named because it focuses on individual enlightenment rather than that of all sentient beings. The Hinayana comprises the foundational Buddhist teachings of the Shravakayana and Pratyekabuddhayana. It emphasizes monastic discipline, strict meditation, contemplation of the Four Noble Truths, renunciation of the worldly distractions of samsara, and rigorous study of the twelve links of dependent origination, all of which eventually bring about the realization of the emptiness of self and thereby liberation from cyclic existence. See also **arhat, Buddhadharma, dependent origination, emptiness,** and **Mahayana**.

hungry ghost (Tib. *yid dag*): Disembodied bardo beings who are tormented by tremendous craving, hunger, and thirst.

inner tantras (Tib. *nang rgyud*): According to the nine-yana scheme of the Nyingma school, the esoteric, tantric teachings of the Buddha are dividied into outer and inner aspects. The outer tantras empower us to fully connect to and embody our buddha nature by emphasizing outer supports like body postures, purification practices, and rituals. The inner tantras enable us to fully recognize and manifest our enlightened nature instantaneously, and from that realization, outer activities like ritual become expressions of one's enlightened activity. See **yana**.

kama lineage (Tib. *ring brgyud bka' ma*): *Kama* refers to the teachings or transmitted precepts that are part of an unbroken oral lineage that passes from master to disciple. The kama lineage is the lifeblood of the Nyingma teachings since it entails the continuous and uninterrupted living transmission of Dharma from teacher to student that stretches all the way back to Buddha Shakyamuni and the primordial buddha, Samantabhadra. His Holiness Dudjom Rinpoche discusses the importance of this transmission lineage: "The teachings that were passed on from mouth to ear in unbroken succession from Buddha Samantabhadra up to your own root lama are known as the long lineage of kama. . . . From the sutra point of view, they contain vinaya and bodhisattva teachings. From the tantra point of view they contain kriya, upa, and yoga teachings. And from the extraordinary Nyingma point of view they contain three inner tantra teachings: Mahayoga, Anuyoga, and Atiyoga. . . . The kama teaching is the foundation and heart of the Nyingma School, and from ancient times it spread beautifully in Tibet. Study the religious history of the Nyingma School and the biographies of its masters, and you will see why the Nyingma kama tradition is so important." See also **Nyingma**.

karma (Tib. *las*): Literally, "action" or "activity," *karma* generally refers to volitional action in which virtuous actions give rise to positive results and negative actions give rise to negative results. Karma is often classified as either individual or collective. As the *Rangjung Yeshe Tibetan-English Dictionary* explains, "Distinction is made between collective karma, which defines our general perception of the world, and individual karma, which determines our personal experiences." The natural, unerring law of karma, or cause and effect, dictates that all volitional actions are causes that produce like results. Present experiences are largely based on past karma, whereas future experiences are based on both past karma and especially karma created in the present, though when and how karma ripens depends on innumerable causes and conditions.

khenchen (Tib. *mkhan chen*): The online Rigpa Shedra Wiki explains that the term *khenchen* indicates one who has undergone rigorous scholastic training. "Khenchen is a title given to khenpos who show great quality in the way they keep their vows, in their learnedness, and [in] the breadth of their activities for the Dharma. This is a very special distinction not easily given." See also **khenpo**.

khenpo (Tib. *mkhan po*): As the online Rigpa Shedra Wiki explains, "[Khenpo] is a title given in the Nyingma, Sakya, and Kagyu schools to a monk who, after completing a nine-year course in Buddhist philosophy in a shedra, has attained a proven level of knowledge and, in some schools, also of discipline and benevolence. In the Nyingma school, after their studies are completed students are required to teach for a further three years in a shedra before they can be awarded the title of khenpo. It can also refer to the abbot of a monastery and to the preceptor from whom one receives ordination." See also **khenchen** and **shedra**.

lha (Tib. *lha* or *bla*): "Superior body," or "energy body." According to the Tibetan Medicine Education Center, "between the physical body and the mind is the lha body, which develops like a body copy, a shadow or reflection of the physical body. Therefore it is called subtle or energy body." Lha is not physical or mental—it's the power resonance of a person and may remain in the field for a long time. A good person has good energy and a bad person has bad energy.

Longde (Tib. *klong sde*): The "Vast Expanse" section of Dzogchen, one of the three transmission lineages taught primarily by the great translator Vairochana. See **Dzogchen**.

Mahamudra (Tib. *phyag rgya chen po*): Literally, "Great Seal," Mahamudra is a profound Vajrayana practice for directly realizing the buddha nature. It is widely practiced by the Kagyu school of Tibetan Buddhism and corresponds to Dzogchen in the Nyingma school.

mahaparinirvana (Tib. *yongs su myang 'das chen po*): The final passing beyond suffering experienced by buddhas and highly realized masters at the end of their lives.

mahasiddha (Tib. *grub chen*): A accomplished tantric practitioner or adept who has attained supreme siddhi, or extraordinary accomplishment, and is therefore able to demonstrate the insubstantial, dreamlike nature of phenomena by performing activities that appear to be miraculous or even impossible to ordinary beings. See also **siddhi**.

Mahayana (Tib. *theg pa chen po*): Literally, "Great Vehicle," the Mahayana teachings are characterized by the practice of the six paramitas (generosity, discipline, patience, diligence, meditative concentration, and wisdom), the cultivation of the altruistic intention to free all beings from the sufferings of samsara, and the active application of this intention in action or practice. These latter two are respectively known as "aspiring bodhichitta" and "actualizing bodhichitta." Including both sutras and tantras, the Mahayana is generally associated with the second, third, and fourth turnings of the Wheel of Dharma, which emphasize the inseparable union of wisdom (Skt. *prajna*) and compassion (Skt. *karuna*). See also **Hinayana**.

nirmanakaya (Tib. *sprul sku*): Literally, "buddha body of emanation," nirmanakaya is the union of the empty (dharmakaya) and luminous (sambhogakaya) aspects of awareness or reality, which manifests as an unceasing display of wisdom, compassion, and loving-kindness. The term *nirmanakaya* can also refer to the physical emanation of enlightened beings that arises spontaneously and inseparably from the dharmakaya and sambhogakaya. See also **dharmakaya** and **sambhogakaya**.

nirvana (Tib. *myang 'das*): This term is used in various ways in the different levels of Buddhist teaching. Literally, "the state beyond sorrow," *nirvana* generally indicates the realization in which all afflictive mental states that misapprehend reality as it is and thus perpetuate suffering are completely and permanently uprooted. In classical Buddhist literature there are three types of nirvana: (1) with residue, in which a person is still dependent on the karmically conditioned aggregates; (2) without residue, in which the aggregates "have been consumed within emptiness"; and (3) nonabiding nirvana that is free from the extremes of quiescence and cyclic existence. The achievement of the transcendental wisdom rainbow body corresponds to the highest level of enlightenment. See also **samsara**.

Nyingma (Tib. *rnying ma*): Also known as the "Ancient Translation" or "Early Dissemination" school, the word *Nyingma*—literally meaning "ancient ones" or "old ones"—relates to the cycle of Buddhist teachings that was brought from India to Tibet by Shantarakshita, Padmasambhava, King Trisong Detsen, Vimalamitra, Vairochana, and others during the eighth and ninth centuries CE. This school is characterized by its special nine-yana scheme, its profound Dzogchen teachings, and its adherence to the early translations of Buddhist texts introduced and established in Tibet before the so-called New Translation or Later Dissemination schools of Tibetan Buddhism began to develop in the middle of the tenth century and particularly during the eleventh century. The latter include the Kadam-Gelug, the Kagyu, and the Sakya schools. The Nyingma school is transmitted in two principal lineages: the long or distant lineage of *kama* and the short or close lineage of *terma*. See also **Dzogchen**.

Padmasambhava (Tib. *Orgyan Padma 'byung gnas*): Literally, "Lotus-Born," Padmasambhava is also known as Padma Jungne, Padmakara, and Guru Rinpoche, or "Precious Guru." He is an emanation of Buddha Amitabha and Avalokiteshvara, born miraculously on a lotus in Lake Dhanakosha (sometimes called Sindhu Lake) in the land of Oddiyana, northwest of India, four years after the mahaparinirvana of Buddha Shakyamuni. Guru Padmasambhava is the embodiment of all the buddhas of the three times and ten directions and was predicted by Buddha Shakyamuni as the great being who would serve as his regent. He is the buddha who attained the transcendental wisdom rainbow body, an ever-youthful immortal body. In the eighth century, Shantarakshita encouraged King Trisong Detsen to invite Guru Padmasambhava to Tibet in order to subdue the forces that were thwarting the establishment of Buddhadharma there. Considered the "Second Buddha," he is an especially powerful source of refuge during these degenerate times.

phowa (Tib. *'pho ba*): Known simply as "transference," the yogic practice of phowa entails transferring one's consciousness to a higher state at the moment of death; this practice should only be performed when all other attempts to prolong one's life have failed. The Venerable Rinpoches teach five kinds of phowa. The first type is the highest phowa, the dharmakaya phowa, which strengthens the view. The second is the sambhogakaya phowa, which unites the visualization and dissolution practices. The third type is the nirmanakaya phowa of immeasurable compassion. The fourth one is called the "phowa of the three ideas." These ideas are three objects of focus, or three intentions that we maintain in the practice. First, we see our consciousness as the traveler; it's our consciousness that is migrating. Second, the central channel is the passage or highway. Third, our destination or home is Dewachen, the pureland of Buddha Amitabha. During phowa practice, we visualize our consciousness traveling on the highway to our home. The fifth phowa is done to benefit others and is called the "forceful phowa that supports the dead" or the "phowa that is a compassionate support for others."

rainbow body (Tib. *ja lu*): The achievement of the transcendental wisdom rainbow body—an ever-youthful immortal body—corresponds to the highest level of enlightenment, where the physical body completely dissolves into wisdom energies signified by different colored lights at the time of death.

rigpa (Tib. *rig pa*): In general, Buddhist teachings use the Tibetan term *rigpa* to indicate conceptual knowledge or understanding, whereas the Dzogchen teachings use it more specifically to indicate the intrinsic awareness that is nonconceptual wisdom. As the Venerable Rinpoches explain, rigpa has the three characteristics of emptiness, clarity, and unceasing energy. The emptiness aspect of rigpa is dharmakaya; the clarity or brightness aspect of rigpa is sambhogakaya; and the unceasing compassionate energy of rigpa is nirmanakaya. See also **emptiness**, **dharmakaya**, **sambhogakaya**, **nirmanakaya**, and **Dzogchen**.

rinpoche (Tib. *rin po che*): Literally, "precious" or "precious one," this is an honorific title accorded the seniormost lamas of the Tibetan Buddhist tradition. It can indicate a tulku, or the conscious reincarnation of a previous master, but is often used as a courteous title.

sadhana (Tib. *sgrub thabs*): This term is used for both a tantric practice sequence and the text on which it is based. It always includes the "Three Noble Ones" of (1) refuge and bodhichitta, (2) creation stage visualization and completion stage dissolution, and (3) the recitation of dedication and aspiration prayers.

sambhogakaya (Tib. *Longs spyod rdzogs pa'I sku*): Literally, the "buddha body of complete enjoyment," sambhogakaya is the energy, clarity, and vitality of one's own innate awareness, or dharmakaya; it is the spontaneously accomplished and inherent richness of wisdom. From the emptiness of the dharmakaya, the sambhogakaya manifests at a very subtle level and is usually perceived only by those with a very high degree of realization. Although one can speak of the three kayas as separate things, they are ultimately indivisible. See also **dharmakaya** and **nirmanakaya**.

samsara (Tib. *khor wa*): Samsara is characterized by fundamental ignorance, afflictive mental states, and karma. These arise in conjunction with the twelve links of interdependent origination. Sentient beings take birth somewhere in the six realms and inevitably experience old age, sickness, death, and rebirth. Fundamentally, samsara does not exist outside of mind since it is nothing other than delusion—the failure to recognize the nature of reality as it is. From this perspective, not recognizing the true nature is samsara, while recognizing the true nature is nirvana. See **nirvana**.

sangha (Tib. *dge 'dun*): The sangha is the last of the Three Jewels in which a practitioner takes refuge. Broadly speaking, this term refers to students of the Dharma or spiritual friends of four types: (1) monks, (2) nuns, (3) lay male practitioners, and (4) lay female practitioners. Specifically, the "noble sangha" is comprised of those who have achieved the first bhumi (the path of seeing) and beyond. See also **buddha**, **Dharma**, **Three Jewels**, and **Three Roots**.

Seven Line Prayer (Tib. *tshig bdun gsol 'debs*): The Seven Line Prayer to Guru Padmasambhava is renowned as one of the most powerful and extraordinary prayers of Tibetan Buddhism. It is mantra, or sacred sound, encompassing all the prayers we do. Generally speaking, this beautiful prayer includes refuge and bodhichitta, invocation, joy, appreciation, and determination. As practitioners of the Nyingma lineage we say this three times at the beginning of all our practice sessions. See also **Nyingma**.

shedra: A center for learning and study of Buddhism. The online Rigpa Wiki says, "In traditional monastic centres, the shedra is the school where monks and nuns study the most important Buddhist scriptures, based on the explanations of their teacher, or khenpo." See also **khenpo**.

siddhi (Tib. *dngos grub*): Often translated as "accomplishment" or "fruit," *siddhis* can be of the common or supreme variety. "Common siddhis" refer to achieving nonliberative supernatural powers such as the ability to read the minds of others, fly, or remember everything one hears in exact detail (i.e., perfect recall). Among the most famous of this variety are the "eight common siddhis related with substances" (Tib. *dngos grub brgyad*). These eight include (1) sword, (2) eye medicine, (3) wind-walking, or speed feet, (4) invisibility, (5) "seeing," or omniscience, (6) extracting the essence, (7) traveling to celestial realms, and (8) traveling to sacred, hidden lands. In contrast, the "supreme siddhi" indicates the achievement of full enlightenment.

stupa (Tib. *mchod rten*): A reliquary monument that generally represents the enlightened mind of the buddhas. As Venerable Khenpo Tsewang Dongyal Rinpoche explains in the 2006 fall issue of *Pema Mandala*, "Stupas benefit both visible and invisible beings, and the world as a whole. They balance and store up the power and energy of the elements and release that power into the environment in a timely fashion, like a satellite." He emphasizes that stupas are very helpful to both invisible beings and those beings we can directly perceive, and that they lessen warfare and disease.

tantra (Tib. *rgyud*): The Sanskrit word *tantra* literally means "continuity" or "continuum." As the Venerable Rinpoches explain, "What is continuing? In the context of the Guhyagarbha Tantra, the profound and beautiful qualities of the inherent richness nature of each and every being is continuing. This nature continues without any interruption whatsoever, regardless of the external changes we go through related with circumstances and situations. External changes never affect the continuity of the reality nature we all share." And as the Rangjung Yeshe Wiki explains, "[*Tantra* refers to] the Vajrayana teachings given by the Buddha in his sambhogakaya form. The real sense of tantra is 'continuity,' the innate buddha nature, which is known as the 'tantra of the expressed meaning.' The general sense of *tantra* is the extraordinary tantric scriptures, also known as the 'tantra of the expressing words.' Can also refer to all the resultant teachings of Vajrayana as a whole." See also **Vajrayana**.

terma: The word *terma*, or "hidden treasure," refers to secret teachings that were concealed throughout Tibet, Nepal, and Bhutan, and even in the mindstreams of disciples, by Guru Padmasambhava, Yeshe Tsogyal, Vimalamitra, and others, principally during the eighth and ninth centuries. Termas were to be revealed at a later prophesied time by destined practitioners known as *tertons*, who are reincarnations of the twenty-five principal disciples of Guru Padmasambhava. As His Holiness Dudjom Rinpoche explains, "Foreseeing the degeneration of the teachings and beings in times to come, Guru Rinpoche kindly hid an inconceivable number of treasure troves containing the dharma, wealth, blessing substances, and so forth in glaciers, rocky mountains, lakes, and many other places. When the time was right, tertons [treasure revealers] emanated, opened the treasure doors, and spread the teachings they contained. These teachings then are known as the close lineage of the termas. This lineage comprises inconceivable pith instructions, yogic activities, and ritual practices of the creation and completion stages." Many great lineage masters describe three general kinds of terma: (1) earth or land terma; (2) mind terma; and (3) pure vision terma. See also **kama lineage** and **Nyingma**.

thigle (Skt. *bindu*; Tib. *thig le*): Literally, "circle," "sphere," "point," or "drop," this term has many meanings depending on the context. Sometimes translated as "seminal point," *thigle* can alternately refer to (1) the white and red essence elements of the body; (2) the dharmakaya (the "unique seminal point"); or (3) the lights that appear during togal visions. The supreme thigle resides in the heart center and is considered to be the seed of buddhahood from the perspective of tantra. It is the size of a small pea or mustard seed, incorporating the pure essences of the five elements in its glowing five colors of blue, white, red, green, and yellow. A very subtle vital energy (wind) dwells in this pea-sized five-colored sphere, and at the time of death the white essence (from the father) descends from the crown, while the red essence (from the mother) ascends from around the genitals. After meeting and joining in the supreme thigle in the heart, these two essence elements dissolve. This dissolution corresponds to the time of death and the cessation of inner respiration, which is immediately followed by the dawning of inner radiance in the bardo of the true nature. See also **togal**.

Three Jewels (Skt. *Triratna*; Tib. *Dkon Mchog Gsum*): Referring to the Buddha, the Dharma, and the Sangha, a Buddhist practitioner takes refuge in the Three Jewels, which offer protection from the endless sufferings and confusion of samsara. Although in this case "the Buddha" refers to the historical Buddha Shakyamuni, on a more subtle level the Buddha represents the nature of reality and the nature of the five kayas and five wisdoms. "The Dharma" is the teachings, the words, names, and letters used to convey the holy instructions of the Noble Ones. And "the Sangha," or community of practitioners, includes the *actual* sangha of realized beings—those who have minimally achieved the path of seeing—and the *resembling* sangha of practitioners still on the path of accumulation or joining. His Holiness Dudjom Rinpoche explains the inner meaning of the Three Jewels: "Externally, the Buddha is the guide, the source of Dharma; the Dharma is the path that Buddha showed; and the Sangha members are the people whose minds are turned toward the Dharma. The Buddha, Dharma, and Sangha also exist internally and symbolically as a profound and skillful way to lead us out of samsara. From the point of view of absolute truth, even the Buddha, Dharma, and Sangha are within us. Our mind is empty, radiant and aware, and that is the precious Buddha. Externally, the Dharma manifests as words and meaning that are heard and practiced, but internally the Dharma is the empty, unobstructed, and self-luminous display of *rigpa*, or nondual awareness. Externally, the followers of the Dharma are the Sangha, but internally the Sangha is the all-pervading, all-encompassing quality of the mind. The three jewels are inherent within us, but since we do not recognize this, we take refuge externally in the Buddha, Dharma, and Sangha with devotion." See also **buddha**, **Buddhadharma**, **sangha**, and **Three Roots**.

Three Roots (Tib. *rtsa ba gsum*): The Three Roots are (1) the lama (Skt. *guru*; Tib. *bla ma*) or Vajrayana teacher, who is the source of blessings; (2) the yidam (Skt. *deva*; Tib. *yi dam*), or tutelary deity, who is the source of siddhis; and (3) the khandros or dakinis (Tib. *mkha' 'gro*), who are the source of fulfillment of beneficial activities. The Vajrayana teachings often state that for those who weren't alive during the time of the Buddha, the guru is in fact *kinder* than the Buddha, since he or she actually embodies the Buddha, Dharma, and Sangha, introduces one to the nature of mind, and maintains and upholds an unbroken lineage tradition that is directly passed on to disciples. See also **Three Jewels**.

togal (Tib. *lhun grub thod rgal*): This "leaping over" technique of Dzogchen emphasizes the luminous aspect of awareness that precedes the duality of samsara and nirvana. In the practice of togal, one abides in the trekcho state, allowing one's inner wisdom to manifest externally as spontaneous visions of the nature as it is. As the Venerable Rinpoches explain, "By abiding uninterruptedly in the state of rigpa without grasping [on] to anything that arises, one will gradually progress through the experiences of the four visions [of togal]. Through properly combining the practices of trekcho and togal with respect, humility, and honor toward the lineage and lineage masters, one can achieve liberation during life, at the moment of death, or in the bardo. The ultimate fruition of successful togal practice is the achievement of the transcendental wisdom rainbow body." See also **Dzogchen** and **trekcho**.

torma (Tib. *gtor ma*): Tormas are ritual sculptures of various shapes formed with butter and *tsampa* (roasted barley), which serve as symbols on many different levels. They may signify the outer cosmic mandala, the inner deity mandala, the deities themselves, all objects of sensual pleasure, the hand objects of the deities, and so forth. Traditionally, tormas are commonly offered to the deities during ritual practices and ceremonies.

trekcho (Tib. *ka dag khregs chod*): Literally "thorough cut" or "cutting through resistance," trekcho is a special method of Dzogchen that emphasizes the recognition of the primordial purity of all phenomena. It is also described simply as "resting in the nature of mind." As the Venerable Rinpoches explain, "The nature of mind is the *kadak* state of primordial purity, or trekcho awareness. In the practice of cutting thoroughly, we are trying to rest our minds in the present state without being disturbed by conceptual fabrications and emotions. Succeeding in this, we will soon discover that our minds are free from the three times of past, present, and future: The past is gone, the future has not yet arrived, and the present is always changing. Therefore, we have to rest in the fourth time, which is actually rigpa, or the original state of present wakefulness. All thoughts are displays of our own rigpa that naturally dissolve back into the true nature if we do not chase after them with attachment, acceptance, or rejection. Trekcho refers to cutting through every aspect of grasping, clinging, hope, and fear. We instantly cut through each concept, each expectation, preference, and emotional fabrication—everything is released and liberated in the natural state. . . . But these are absolute-level teachings to be followed when one can consistently maintain that level of realization. In order to achieve this realization of the lineage teachings, the practice of skillful means is extremely important. Therefore, the teachings repeatedly say that skillful means and wisdom always go together. In Dzogchen terminology, this is described as the union of awareness and emptiness. Additionally, Dzogchen is also the union of appearance and emptiness, and the accumulation of both wisdom and merit. By using these relative methods, we are going to reveal the naked nature as it is." See also **Dzogchen**, **rigpa**, and **togal**.

tsok (Skt. *ganachakra*; Tib. *tshogs*): Tsok is a tantric ritual feast offering consisting of four assemblages: (1) the fortunate gathering of devotees; (2) the luxurious abundance of offerings; (3) the deities who are the joyous recipients; and proceeding from these three, (4) the deep accumulation of merit and wisdom. Among the many practices of skillful means, tsok is one of the most powerful, as described by the Venerable Rinpoches: "The great master Jamgön Kongtrul Rinpoche says that the ganachakra offering is one of the greatest ways to increase merit. This was taught by the Buddha many times in different tantras, especially the Tantra of the Glorious Wheel of Lightning. . . . The Buddha explained that the ganachakra offering and tsok ceremonies are extremely powerful. Kongtrul Yonten Gyatso adds that there are not many people who can truly perform and enjoy the ganachakra ceremony in this age, at this time. There are many instructions on how to properly perform the ganachakra. However, even if you don't have the capability to fully engage in this practice, if you gather the offerings and perform the ceremony according to your capabilities, with devotion and meditation, that offering will be very special. It will purify obscurations, remove obstacles, and increase realization. These ceremonies should be performed on the tenth and twenty-fifth days of the lunar calendar, or the waxing and waning tenth days." See also **Vajrayana**.

Vajrayana (Tib. *rdo rje'i theg pa*): The Vajrayana is also known as the "Adamantine Vehicle," the "Indestructible Vehicle," the "Secret Mantrayana" (Skt. *Guhyamantra*; Tib. *gsang ngags kyi theg pa*), and "Mantrayana." The latter two names indicate that mind is protected from dualistic conceptions through the practice of this vehicle; in the Sanskrit word *mantra*, the root *mana* can be translated as "mind," and the suffix *tra* can be translated as "protection." On one level, the Vajrayana is referred to as "secret" because it has traditionally been transmitted from a qualified teacher to a qualified disciple and kept hidden from those who would misinterpret the teachings and thereby harm themselves and others. However, on a deeper level, this secret quality alludes to the "self-secret" nature of awareness that remains hidden from duality mind. There are two very important foundational elements to all Vajrayana practice: (1) a vast and sincere motivation of bodhichitta, which is the strong wish to bring all sentient beings, without partiality, to the state of complete enlightenment; and (2) a pure understanding or view of the true nature, which regards all phenomena—including one's own aggregates—as the pervasive wisdom display of the "three vajra states" (Tib. *rdo rje gsum*), the inseparable union of wisdom and compassion. Within this context, the Vajrayana is characterized by innumerable tantric techniques such as visualization, mantra recitation, and various yogic disciplines, all of which are designed to bring every aspect of experience—including the eight consciousnesses, all mental events, the five poisons, and the six bardos—to the path of Dharma. This is ultimately accomplished by stabilizing recognition of the nature of mind, which is the primordial union of appearance and emptiness, or wisdom and compassion. In general, the Vajrayana (i.e., Buddhist tantra) is said to have ten characteristics, which are listed by Namkhai Norbu Rinpoche as follows: (1) outlook/view, (2) meditation, (3) behavior/conduct, (4) initiation/empowerment, (5) mandala, (6) charismatic activity, (7) commitments/samayas, (8) capacities, (9) worship, and (10) mantra. These diverse methods use the dynamic power of mental, physical, and verbal activities to transcend and transform mundane habit patterns into their corresponding wisdom nature. For instance, the five poisons are ultimately experienced as the five wisdoms. Through the skillful means of the Vajrayana, a practitioner uses the previously overwhelming power of the negativities and defilements to connect with the primordial purity of both awareness and phenomena, of subject, object, and action. The Nyingma school divides the Vajrayana teachings into three outer tantras (Kriyatantra, Upatantra, and Yogatantra) and three inner tantras (Mahayoga, Anuyoga, and Atiyoga). In contrast with the "causal" teachings of the Sutrayana, which approach enlightenment by gradually removing what is temporarily obscuring the buddha nature, the Vajrayana teachings are known as "resultant" because "the indestructible and imperishable realities of Buddha's body, speech, and mind are fully realized and manifested when the continuum of the ground is transformed into the continuum of the result by means of the continuum of the path." In other words, when the *alaya* (Tib. *kun gzhi*, i.e., the ground) is purified of dualistic conceptions, karmic imprints, and obscurations by practicing on all forms, sounds, and thoughts as the wisdom display of awareness through the various techniques of the Secret Mantra (i.e., the path), body, speech, and mind are realized and manifest as the displays of enlightenment, none other than the shining qualities of one's own innate nature (i.e., the result). Hence, the ground and the result are essentially identical: the *ground* is primordial awareness, the inherent, original nature of tantra that is the indestructible, unborn true nature; and the *result* is complete recognition and understanding of this nature as an unbroken, vivid experience that transcends the duality of subject, object, and action. This true nature of reality—primordial, nondual awareness, or the innermost nature of mind itself—is known as *rigpa* in Dzogchen terminology. See **rigpa**.

yana (Tib. *theg pa dgu*): According to the Nyingma school of Tibetan Buddhism, the 84,000 teachings of the Buddha can all be summarized in terms of the nine yanas, or "vehicles." They are: (1) Shravakayana, or "Hearer Vehicle"; (2) Pratyekabuddhayana, or "Solitary Realizer Vehicle"; (3) Bodhisattvayana, or "Bodhisattva Vehicle"; (4) Kriyayogatantra, or "Action Yoga Tantra"; (5) Upayogatantra, or "Dual Yoga Tantra"; (6) Yogayogatantra, or "Yoga Tantra"; (7) Mahayogatantra, or "Great Yoga Tantra"; and (8) Anuyogatantra, or "Subsequent Yoga Tantra"; (9) Atiyogatantra, or "Supreme Yoga Tantra." According to the Nyingma classification, the first two yanas are known as "foundational Buddhism," or "Hinayana," and all the rest of the yanas—from the third through the ninth—are known as "Mahayana." The Vajrayana, also known as "Tantrayana," includes everything from Kriyayoga (the fourth yana) up to and including Atiyoga (the ninth). Yanas four through six—Kriyayoga, Upayoga, and

Yogayoga—comprise the outer tantras, while yanas seven through nine—Mahayoga, Anuyoga, and Atiyoga—make up the inner tantras.

yidam (Skt. *deva*; Tib. *yi dam*): A yidam, or tutelary deity, is the source of siddhis, or accomplishments. See **deity** and **siddhi**.

Zhitro (Tib. *zhi khro*): The Tibetan term *Zhitro* can be translated into English as "Peaceful and Wrathful Deities" or "Peaceful and Wrathful Ones," and generally refers to a cycle of teachings that belongs to the inner tantras. Specifically, these are condensed instructions based on the fundamental meaning of the Guhyagarbha Tantra (Tib. *gsang ba'i snying po*), combined with the views expressed in the Anuyoga and Atiyoga tantras. So the Zhitro teachings are the essence of the Guhyagarbha Tantra at the level of practice; we could say they are the pith (essential) instructions of the Guhyagarbha Tantra, the "King of All Tantras." Therefore, meditating on the peaceful and wrathful deities is an easy and condensed way to engage in this profound tantra. Many great masters have described the Zhitro teachings as the "inner tantra of the inner tantras." Here we are not making distinctions between the various inner tantras, nor between the creation and completion stages, but we are joining them together. This is the union of rigpa and emptiness, the oneness of birth, death, and life experiences. There is no basis for discriminating between this and that, subject and object, because all are aspects of the one true nature. We are not rejecting or accepting anything exclusively. For this reason, Zhitro is known as a teaching that unifies everything in a single state.

Index

About the Authors

VEN. KHENCHEN PALDEN SHERAB RINPOCHE
(1938–2010)

Venerable Khenchen Palden Sherab Rinpoche was a renowned scholar and meditation master of the Nyingma school of Tibetan Buddhism. He was born on May 10, 1938, in the Doshul region of Kham in eastern Tibet, near the sacred mountain Jowo Zegyal. On the morning of his birth a small snow fell with flakes in the shape of lotus petals. Among his ancestors were many great scholars, practitioners, and tertons.

Photograph by Debi Harbin, 2000

His family was seminomadic, living in the village during the winter and moving with the herds to high mountain pastures in the summer, where they lived in yak-hair tents. The monastery for the Doshul region is known as Gochen Monastery, founded by the great terton Tsasum Lingpa, and his father's family had the hereditary responsibility for administering the business affairs of the monastery. His grandfather had been both administrator and chant master, in charge of ritual ceremonies.

Khenchen Rinpoche began his education at Gochen Monastery at age four. He entered Riwoche Monastery at age fourteen, completing his studies there just before the Chinese invasion of Tibet reached the area. Among his root teachers was the illustrious Khenchen Tenzin Dragpa (Katok Khenpo Ashe).

In 1959, Khenchen Rinpoche and his family were forced into exile, escaping to India. After a tumultuous period following their escape, in 1967 he was appointed head of the Nyingma department of the Central Institute of Higher Tibetan Studies in Sarnath by His Holiness Dudjom Rinpoche, the supreme head of the Nyingma school of Tibetan Buddhism. He held the position of abbot for seventeen years, dedicating all his time and energy to ensure the survival and spread of the Buddha's teachings.

Venerable Khenchen Palden Sherab Rinpoche moved to the United States in 1984 to work closely with His Holiness Dudjom Rinpoche. In 1985, he and his brother, Venerable Khenpo Tsewang Dongyal Rinpoche, founded the Dharma Samudra Publishing Company. In 1988 they founded the Padmasambhava Buddhist Center (PBC), which has centers throughout the United States as well as in Puerto Rico, Russia, and India, among other countries. The principal center is Palden Padma Samye Ling, located in Delaware County, upstate New York. PBC also includes a traditional Tibetan Buddhist monastery and nunnery at the holy site of Deer Park in Sarnath, and the Miracle Stupa for World Peace at Padma Samye Jetavan, which is in Jetavan Grove in Shravasti, India.

Khenchen Rinpoche traveled extensively in the United States and throughout the world, giving teachings and empowerments, conducting retreats and seminars, and establishing meditation centers. He authored three volumes of Tibetan works and coauthored over thirty-five books in English with Venerable Khenpo Tsewang Dongyal Rinpoche.

His collected Tibetan works include the following:

Advice from the Ancestral Vidyadhara, a commentary on Padmasambhava's *Stages of the Path, Heap of Jewels*

Blazing Clouds of Wisdom and Compassion, a commentary on the hundred-syllable mantra of Vajrasattva

Clouds of Blessings, an explanation of prayers to Terchen Tsasum Lingpa, and other learned works, poems, prayers and sadhanas

The Essence of Diamond Clear Light, an outline and structural analysis of *The Aspiration Prayer of Samantabhadra*

The Mirror of Mindfulness, an explanation of the six bardos

Opening the Eyes of Wisdom, a commentary on Sangye Yeshe's *Lamp of the Eye of Contemplation*

Opening the Door of Blessings, a biography of Machig Labdron

The Ornament of Stars at Dawn, an outline and structural analysis of Vasubandhu's *Twenty Verses*

The Ornament of Vairochana's Intention, a commentary on the *Heart Sutra Lotus Necklace of Devotion*, a biography of Khenchen Tenzin Dragpa

Pleasure Lake of Nagarjuna's Intention, a general summary of Madhyamaka

The Radiant Light of the Sun and Moon, a commentary on Mipham Rinpoche's *The Sword of Wisdom That Ascertains Reality*

The Smile of Sun and Moon: A Commentary on the Praise to the Twenty-One Taras

Smiling Red Lotus, a short commentary on the prayer to Yeshe Tsogyal

Supreme Clear Mirror, an introduction to Buddhist logic

Waves of the Ocean of Devotion, a biography-praise to Nubchen Sangye Yeshe, and *Vajra Rosary*, biographies of his main incarnations

White Lotus, an explanation of prayers to Guru Rinpoche

VEN. KHENPO TSEWANG DONGYAL RINPOCHE
(1950–)

Venerable Khenpo Tsewang Dongyal Rinpoche was born in the Dhoshul region of Kham in eastern Tibet on June 10, 1950. On that summer day in the family tent, Rinpoche's birth caused his mother, Pema Lhadze, no pain. The next day, upon moving the bed where she had delivered the baby, his mother found growing a beautiful and fragrant flower that she plucked and offered to Chenrezig on the family altar. Soon after Khenpo Tsewang was born, three head lamas from Jadchag Monastery came to his home and recognized him as the reincarnation of Khenpo Sherab Khyentse, who had been the former head abbot at Gochen Monastery. Sherab Khyentse was a renowned scholar and practitioner who spent much of his life in retreat.

Khenpo Rinpoche began his formal schooling at the age of five, when he entered Gochen monastery. However, his first Dharma teacher was his father, Lama Chimed Namgyal Rinpoche. The Chinese invasion of Tibet interrupted his studies, and he escaped to India with his family in 1959. There his father and brother, Khenchen Rinpoche, continued his education until he entered the Nyingmapa Monastic School of Northern India, where he studied until 1967. Khenpo Rinpoche then entered the Central Institute of Higher Tibetan Studies, which at the time was a part of Sanskrit University in Varanasi, where he received his

Photograph by Debi Harbin, 2000

BA degree in 1975. He also attended Nyingmapa University in West Bengal, where he received another BA and an MA in 1977.

In 1978, His Holiness Dudjom Rinpoche enthroned Venerable Khenpo Tsewang Dongyal Rinpoche as the abbot of the Wish-Fulfilling Nyingmapa Institute in Boudanath, Nepal, where he taught poetry, grammar, and philosophy. Then in 1981, His Holiness appointed Khenpo Rinpoche as the abbot of the Dorje Nyingpo center in Paris, France. Finally, in 1982, he asked Khenpo Tsewang to work with him at the Yeshe Nyingpo center in New York City. During that time until His Holiness Dudjom Rinpoche's mahaparinirvana in 1987, Khenpo Rinpoche continued to work closely with him, often traveling with His Holiness as his translator and attendant.

In 1988, Khenpo Tsewang and his brother, Venerable Khenchen Palden Sherab Rinpoche, founded the Padmasambhava Buddhist Center (PBC). Since that time he has served as a spiritual director at the various PBC centers throughout the world. He maintains an active traveling and teaching schedule.

Khenpo Tsewang is the author of *Light of Fearless Indestructible Wisdom: The Life and Legacy of His Holiness Dudjom Rinpoche* (Shambhala, 2008), published in both Tibetan and English. He has also authored a book of poetry on the life of Guru Rinpoche entitled *Praise to the Lotus Born: A Verse Garland of Waves of Devotion* (Dharma Samudra, 2004), and a unique two-volume cultural and religious history of Tibet titled *Expressing the Six Distinctive Greatnesses of the Ancient School by Recalling the Kind Legacy of the Great Masters, Translators, and Dharma Kings Known as "Rejoicing Laughter of the Noble Beings"* (Dharma Samudra, 2020), which details the historical bases of the Dharma in Tibet from the sixth through ninth centuries. At present this is one of the only books yet written that conveys the Dharma activities of this historical period in such depth, and His Holiness Dudjom Rinpoche encouraged Khenpo Tsewang to complete it, describing the work as an important contribution to the history of the kama lineage.

Along with these, Venerable Khenpo Tsewang Dongyal Rinpoche has coauthored over thirty-five Dharma books in English with Venerable Khenchen Palden Sherab Rinpoche.

Books and Publications by the Authors

PADMA SAMYE LING SHEDRA SERIES

The complete Padma Samye Ling Shedra Series includes eight books by the Venerable Khenpo Rinpoches that cover their Shedra teachings from 2003–2009 at Padma Samye Ling Monastery and Retreat Center in upstate New York, as well as an overview on all of the nine yanas that Venerable Khenchen Palden Sherab Rinpoche gave in Australia in 1987.

(Vol. 1) *Opening the Clear Vision of the Vaibhashika and Sautrantika Schools* (Dharma Samudra, 2007)

(Vol. 2) *Opening the Clear Vision of the Mind Only School* (Dharma Samudra, 2007)

(Vol. 3) *Opening the Wisdom Door of the Madhyamaka School* (Dharma Samudra, 2007)

(Vol. 4) *Opening the Wisdom Door of the Rangtong and Shentong Views: A Brief Explanation of the One Taste of the Second and Third Turning of the Wheel of Dharma* (Dharma Samudra, 2007)

(Vol. 5) *Opening the Wisdom Door of the Outer Tantras: Refining Awareness Through Ascetic Ritual and Purification Practice* (Dharma Samudra, 2008)

(Vol. 6) *Turning the Wisdom Wheel of the Nine Golden Chariots* (Dharma Samudra, 2009)

(Vol. 7) *Splendid Presence of the Great Guhyagarbha: Opening the Wisdom Door of the King of All Tantras* (Dharma Samudra, 2011)

(Vol. 8) *Key to Opening the Wisdom Door of Anuyoga: Exploring the One Taste of the Three Mandalas* (Dharma Samudra, 2015)

OTHER PUBLICATIONS BY THE AUTHORS

Advice from a Spiritual Friend: A Commentary on Nagarjuna's Letter to a Friend (Dharma Samudra, 2019)

The Beauty of Awakened Mind: Dzogchen Lineage of the Great Master Shigpo Dudtsi (Dharma Samudra, 2018)

The Buddhist Path: A Practical Guide from the Nyingma Tradition of Tibetan Buddhism (formerly titled *Opening to Our Primordial Nature*) (Snow Lion, 2010)

Ceaseless Echoes of the Great Silence: A Commentary on the Heart Sutra Prajnaparamita (English and Spanish) (Dharma Samudra, 2012)

Cutting Through Ego and Revealing Fearlessness: Chod Practice According to Jigme Lingpa's Bellowing Laugh of the Dakini (Dharma Samudra, 2019)

The Dark Red Amulet: Oral Instructions on the Practice of Vajrakilaya Discovering Infinite Freedom: The Prayer of Küntuzangpo (Snow Lion, 2009)

Door to Inconceivable Wisdom and Compassion (Sky Dancer Press, 1999)

The Essential Journey of Life and Death, Volume I: Indestructible Nature of Body, Speech, and Mind; and *Volume II: Using Dream Yoga and Phowa as the Path* (Dharma Samudra, 2012)

Expressing the Six Distinctive Greatnesses of the Ancient School by Recalling the Kind Legacy of the Great Masters, Translators, and Dharma Kings: Known as "Rejoicing Laughter of the Noble Beings" (in Tibetan; Dharma Samudra, 2020)

Heart Essence of Chetsun: Voice of the Lion (restricted) (Dharma Samudra, 2007)

Illuminating the Path: Ngondro Instructions According to the Nyingma School of Vajrayana Buddhism (English and Spanish; Padmasambhava Buddhist Center, 2008)

Inborn Realization: A Commentary on His Holiness Dudjom Rinpoche's Mountain Retreat Instructions (Dharma Samudra, 2016)

Liberating Duality with Wisdom Display: The Eight Manifestations of Guru Padmasambhava (Dharma Samudra, 2013)

Light of Fearless Indestructible Wisdom: The Life and Legacy of His Holiness Dudjom Rinpoche (Shambhala, 2008)

Light of Peace: How Buddhism Shines in the World Lion's Gaze: A Commentary on the Tsig Sum Nedek (Dharma Samudra, 2019)

Mipham's Sword of Wisdom: The Nyingma Approach to Valid Cognition (Wisdom Publications, 2018)

The Nature of Mind (formerly titled *Pointing Out the Nature of Mind: Dzogchen Pith Instructions of Aro Yeshe Jungne*) (Snow Lion, 2016)

Prajnaparamita: The Six Perfections (Sky Dancer, 1991)

Praise to the Lotus Born: A Verse Garland of Waves of Devotion (Dharma Samudra, 2004)

The Seven Nails: The Final Testament of the Great Dzogchen Master Shri Singha (Dharma Samudra, 2018)

Smile of Sun and Moon: A Commentary on the Praise to the Twenty-One Taras (Sky Dancer Press, 2004)

Supreme Wisdom: Commentary on Yeshe Lama (restricted) (Sky Dancer, 2004)

Tara's Enlightened Activity: An Oral Commentary on the Twenty-One Praises to Tara (Snow Lion, 2007)

Uprooting Clinging: A Commentary on Mipham Rinpoche's Wheel of Analytic Meditation (Dharma Samudra, 2019)

Vajra Sound of Peace: Practicing the Seven Chapter Prayer of Guru Padmasambhava (Dharma Samudra, 2020)

Walking in the Footsteps of the Buddha: The Path to Freedom (Dharma Samudra, 2019)

OPENING THE DOOR OF THE DHARMA TREASURY PRACTICE GUIDES

The Opening the Door of the Dharma treasury is a series of five practice guides of condensed instructions on some of the main practices of the Padmasambhava Buddhist Center and Nyingma Lineage. Information about these and other works by the Venerable Khenpo Rinpoches can be found online at: www.padmasambhava.org/chiso. The five volumes of the Opening the Door of the Dharma treasury can be found in the Books by Khenpo Rinpoches section under the following listings:

Twelve Deeds of the Buddha commentary (volume 1)

Commentary on the Buddha Sadhana by Mipham Rinpoche (volume 2)

Seven Line Prayer Practice Guide (volume 3)

Four Thoughts that Turn the Mind From Samsara (volume 4)

Vows and Conduct in the Nyingma Tradition (volume 5)

Padmasambhava
Buddhist Center

Venerable Khenchen Palden Sherab Rinpoche and Venerable Khenpo Tsewang Dongyal Rinpoche established Padmasambhava Buddhist Center (PBC) to preserve the authentic message of Buddha Shakyamuni and Guru Padmasambhava in its entirety, and in particular to teach the

Padma Samye Ling Monastery and Retreat Center
Photograph by Kelly Noskov, 2007

199

Nyingma tradition of Vajrayana Buddhism. It is dedicated to world peace and the supreme good fortune and well-being of all. PBC now includes over twenty centers in the United States, Russia, Canada, and Puerto Rico, in addition to monastic institutions in India, Russia, and the United States.

The Samye Translation Group was founded by the Venerable Khenpo Rinpoches to commemorate and preserve the great ancient tradition of translation that was firmly established during the glorious Tibetan Buddhist era of the seventh through tenth centuries. As a reflection of gratitude for the unique activities of these enlightened translators, the Samye Translation Group has published Dharma books that cover all nine yana teachings of the Nyingma school of Tibetan Buddhism, including shedra philosophy books.

For more information about the Venerable Khenpo Rinpoches' activities, the Samye Translation Group, or Padmasambhava Buddhist Center, please contact:

Padma Samye Ling
618 Buddha Highway
Sidney Center, New York 13839
(607) 865-8068
www.padmasambhava.org

Mantra which purifies mishandling a Dharma text.